M.I.T.
in Perspective

M.I.T. in Perspective

A Pictorial History of the
Massachusetts Institute of Technology

by Francis E. Wylie

Little, Brown and Company   Boston   Toronto

FIRST EDITION
T 03/76

The author is grateful to Simon & Schuster, Inc., for permission to quote from *A Trolley to the Moon* by Eric Hodgins. Copyright © 1973 by Eric Hodgins.

Library of Congress Cataloging in Publication Data

Wylie, Francis E.
    M.I.T. in perspective: a pictorial history of the Massachusetts Institute of Technology

    Bibliography: p. 209
    Includes index.
    1. Massachusetts Institute of Technology.   I.   Title.
T171.M49W9   607'.11'7444   75–35888
ISBN 0–316–96200–7

*Published simultaneously in Canada
by Little, Brown & Company (Canada) Limited*

Printed in the United States of America

1 — Frontispiece The area of the campus has not increased nearly as much as the intensity of its use, but now it extends almost to Longfellow Bridge, as marked by Eastgate, the high-rise building for married students. The Green Building, near the center, was the first tall building in Cambridge. In addition to the new buildings, several older, industrial buildings on the fringe of the original campus have been remodeled for use by M.I.T. Skyscrapers have proliferated in Boston, but much of Beacon Hill and Back Bay remains unchanged.

Contents

Foreword

There are two contrasting ways in which a great river can be described. In a scientific approach, exact soundings would be taken, the water would be chemically analyzed, the volume of flow calculated, the fishes and other life described, and so on. In an historical approach, greater attention would be given to the people who inhabited its shores, to the exploits of explorers and boatmen, to the mountains and farmlands through which the river flowed, and to the cities and industries on the banks. Both approaches are valid and, for the layman, the latter provides a more vivid, understandable picture of the character of the river.

In this book, Francis E. Wylie has sought to describe some of the salient features of the stream of history at M.I.T., using pictures extensively to give a feeling for the changes and developments that have occurred, for the educational and scientific accomplishments, and, above all, for a few of the people (there is not room for more) who have played important roles in the evolution of the Institute. The panoramic view that he provides is, I think, an exciting one. Other more detailed and scholarly accounts of M.I.T.'s educational and intellectual progress have been and will be written. Yet this pictorial story of M.I.T. is presented in a manner that is absorbing and contributes very much in its own special way to the comprehension of the Institute's history and character.

Jerome B. Wiesner, President
Massachusetts Institute of Technology

Preface

Oh, back to the days that were free from care
    In the 'ology Varsity shop,
With nothing to do but analyze air
    In an anemometric top;
Or the differentiation of the trigonometrical pow'rs
    Of constant *pi* that made me sigh
    In those happy days of ours.
'Rah for Technology, 'ology, 'ology, oh!

The old days indeed must have been more free from care, for college students sang often and lustily. Tech men loved to sing "Oh give me some 'ology. . . . Any old kind of 'ology," the words by Isaac W. Litchfield '85 to cantering music adapted from "Solomon Levi" by Frederic Field Bullard '87, who also wrote the famous "Stein Song" music — "For it's always fair weather, When good fellows get together." (Bullard threw himself into musical celebration at the 1904 alumni reunion with such intensity that he died three weeks later.)

Singing has gone out of style in recent years and nostalgia is in short supply, perhaps because global and cosmic cares have become so oppressive. All the more reason for looking backward!

M.I.T. is preoccupied with the present and the future rather than the past — one reason it is among the world's great universities. Yet it has a most interesting past, and its history sheds light on the growth of American science, technology, and education during the past century.

This book, with the help of pictures, seeks to tell the story of M.I.T. from its conception to the present in an impressionistic way, without the detail that a scholarly historian would wish to include and with no attempt at careful analysis. Although it refers to most major episodes and 'ologies, space permits only a sampling. In many cases, the choice of samples depended on the availability of appealing pictures, and this availability often depended on the luck that some pictures survived Institute housecleanings and others did not. Selection was painful, and every reader will have different ideas on what should have been included.

Perhaps a hundred thousand people have contributed to the growth of M.I.T. — professors, patrons, administrators, students, alumni, technicians, and so on — and only a few can be represented here. To the others, I can offer only apologies and regrets. M.I.T. tradition calls for definitive studies, be they laboratory reports or ten-volume treatises, and better that they not be done than that they be inadequate. I plead journalist's privilege (and claim merely to be a journalist — not a historian), arguing that a good story is worth telling even though it may not be complete.

Actually, of course, there are many stories, and rather than attempting to weave them into a broad, continuous fabric, as a skillful historian would do, I have taken liberties with chronology and, for more or less logical reasons, have manipulated history to provide self-contained sequences. One will therefore find 1975 pictures mingled with those of 1875.

The author is grateful to many people for their assistance but wishes especially to express appreciation to the four presidents of M.I.T. under whom he has served. Howard W. Johnson, now chairman of the Corporation, happens to be an enthusiast for history, and without his generous interest from the inception of the enterprise this book would not have been possible. James R. Killian Jr., Julius A. Stratton, and Jerome B. Wiesner know far more about M.I.T.'s history, with intimacy and precision, than this writer could ever learn, and they have been most kind. President Wiesner's administrative assistant, Miss Barbara B. Wollan, has made contributions to be explained only in terms of abiding friendship.

The task of assembling material was made immeasurably easier by the formation by Mr. Johnson in 1971 of the Committee for Historical Collections. The chairman, Professor Richard M. Douglas, has been most helpful, and the director of the Historical Collections, Warren A. Seamans, has been imaginative, assiduous, enthusiastic, and tireless in providing pictures and information. With Walter L. Milne, assistant to Mr. Johnson, who played a key role in coordination and counseling, they worked many, many hours in assisting the author with the material in preparation. Professor E. Neal Hartley, Institute archivist, and Miss Eleanor Bartlett, archives librarian, were patient in helping with my quest.

Principal sources of information are listed in the Bibliography except for scores of articles published by *Technology Review,* always a faithful chronicle of M.I.T. history; I thank the current editor, John I. Mattill, and am also indebted to my former colleagues, Robert M. Byers, director of the News Office, William T. Struble, Joanne Miller, and their associates.

Most of the pictures were provided by the Historical Collections but I have given credit to individual photographers where they are known. Two who seldom identified their work, Ralph Jackman and Robert Lyon, made thousands of pictures of which I have doubtless used a number, and I offer a blanket "thanks" to them and to anonymous others. During the past four years, Warren Seamans has achieved a remarkable feat in finding and bringing together paintings, memorabilia, photographs and other historical materials. The majority of the pictures in this book are from the Collections.
— Francis E. Wylie

2   Warren A. Seamans

M.I.T.
in Perspective

1

An Audacious Vision

WILLIAM BARTON ROGERS FOVNDER, carved on the westerly portico of the Massachusetts Institute of Technology, is no perfunctory gesture to its first president. In bold Roman letters above the classical columns, it is a reminder of the audacious concept that still dominates the Institute.

When in 1846 Professor Rogers first set down his ideas for a polytechnic institution, he wrote:

I doubt not that such a nucleus-school would, with the growth of this active and knowledge-seeking community, finally expand into a great institution comprehending the whole field of physical science and the arts with the auxiliary branches of mathematics and modern languages, and would soon overtop the universities of the land in the accuracy and the extent of its teachings in all branches of positive knowledge.

The accuracy of its teachings would be difficult to determine, and M.I.T. makes no claim that it overtops the universities, but it has a formidable reputation which would please Rogers, and he might be astonished at the extent of its program today.

Various ratings by educators confirm the general impression of the Institute's standing. After polling deans of graduate schools, *Change,* a sober education magazine, reported that "M.I.T. is rated as by far the best school of engineering in the nation." Deans of architecture schools ranked M.I.T.'s at the top. Preferences among business school deans placed the Sloan School of Management sixth.

Ratings compiled by the American Council on Education found M.I.T. first in Electrical and Mechanical Engineering and among the leaders in other technical and scientific fields. Furthermore, it was first in Linguistics and first in "effectiveness of doctoral program" in Economics — though second to Harvard in "quality of faculty" in the latter field.

Harvard, just two miles up Massachusetts Avenue in Cambridge, is, to be sure, the greatest university in the world — or at least that was the judgment of international leaders polled by the ubiquitous Mr. Gallup. M.I.T. was ranked below, with Oxford, Cambridge, Princeton, and the Sorbonne. This provided recognition that M.I.T. is indeed a university, though it is a special kind and the extent of its teachings is not as great as Harvard's. It has no school of medicine, of education, or law or of fine arts, yet in recent decades it has demonstrated growing strength in those fields. And it has an excellent School of Humanities and Social Science, with a faculty larger than can be found at many first-rate liberal arts colleges.

William Barton Rogers was one of four remarkable brothers, all of whom became scientists and thus can be compared to the three Compton brothers of a later generation. He attended the College of William and Mary in Virginia, where his father, Dr. Patrick Kerr Rogers, was professor of natural

3   A daguerreotype of William Barton Rogers, recently located and not previously published. The date is uncertain.

4

4   William Barton Rogers (rear) and his wife Emma with her father and brother, James Savage Sr. and Jr. The picture probably was made not long before young Savage, a Union major, went off to the Civil War. Wounded, he was taken to Charlottesville, Virginia, as a prisoner. Rogers wrote to friends there asking them to see that he got special care, but he died.

history and chemistry. Upon his father's death in 1828 he succeeded him in that chair, at the age of twenty-three.

Natural history embraced virtually all of the sciences and young Rogers's interests were broad, but he developed a particular competence in geology. In 1835 he undertook a geological survey of Virginia and that same year he was elected to the professorship of natural philosophy at the University of Virginia, which had been founded by Thomas Jefferson just ten years earlier.

Through eighteen years at the University of Virginia, Rogers was a popular and influential member of the faculty. He was troubled, however, by the atmosphere of anti-intellectualism, manifested by bigotry, student violence, and erratic support by the legislature. Though his geological survey yielded enormously valuable information about coal fields and other natural resources, hard-headed legislators would not appropriate funds for publication of the final report.

The students were infuriated by a rule against carrying firearms on the campus, and when seventy of their number were dismissed for defiance of the rule, they rioted, breaking professors' windows amid "a continual roar of musketry." In other years a professor was horsewhipped and the chairman of the faculty was fatally shot at his door by a masked student. When Rogers was chairman of the faculty, in 1845, riots were so severe that the university had to be closed for a week. Rogers wrote:

Almost every faculty meeting witnesses a suspension or dismission, and this had of course created much heart-burning and awakened some vindictive feeling. Unfortunately we have no way of compelling dismissed students to go home, and hence those from the far South linger for months about the taverns of Charlottesville, rioting in dissipation and tempting away their former associates at the university.

Rogers was distressed by religious intolerance in the community, particularly when the university was attacked in bigoted publications for the appointment of a Roman Catholic and a Jew to the faculty. This occurred at about the time that he went on a geological expedition to New England with his brother Henry. He wrote to another brother, Robert: "Since my summer's rambles with Henry I have been unable to shut out the contrast between the region in which I live and the highly cultivated nature and society of glorious New England."

William and Henry, on various trips, had made many friends in New England and had established scholarly reputations. At a meeting in Boston of the Association of American Geologists and Naturalists they presented a monumental paper describing the structure and formation of the Appalachian Mountains. Each served as chairman of the association, William in 1847 when it voted to reorganize as the American Association for the Advancement of Science.

Henry Rogers, a professor of geology at the University of Pennsylvania, was invited to give the Lowell Institute lectures in Boston in 1844 and decided to remain there, hoping for an appointment to the Harvard faculty (which failed to materialize). The next year, on a trip through the White Mountains, he and William met the family of James Savage, a wealthy and scholarly Bostonian, and soon William Rogers had a special reason for wanting to live in Boston. He married Emma Savage, the eldest daughter, in 1849.

Meanwhile the two brothers had started dreaming about starting a polytechnic school in Boston. In 1846, Henry wrote that he had discussed the possibility with John Amory Lowell, foremost patron of education, and he

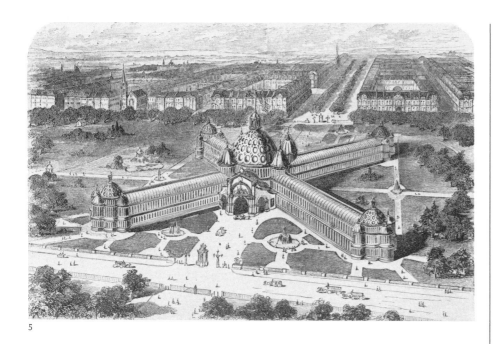

5

5   If the legislature of 1859 had responded to 10,000 signers of a petition, this building in the Public Garden might have been the first home of M.I.T. Historical, fine arts, zoological, and botanical collections were included in the plan, published in the *Conservatory Journal* for promotion of the program.

asked for William's ideas. It was then that William expressed his thoughts about a school that would "overtop the universities of the land." His plan emphasized that such a school would not merely teach technical skills but rather scientific principles as a basis for industrial applications.

"When thus instructed in applied science," William Rogers wrote, "the mechanician, chemist, manufacturer or engineer clearly comprehends the agencies of the materials and instruments with which he works, and is, therefore, saved from the disasters of blind experiment, is guided securely because understandingly in a profitable routine, and is directed in the contrivance of new and more combinations."

John Lowell turned down the proposal but the two brothers continued to develop their ideas. William resigned from the University of Virginia in 1853 and he and his wife moved to Boston. Four years later, Henry Rogers accepted a professorship at the University of Glasgow, leaving William to pursue their dream.

The intellectual capital of America, Boston was devoted to such literary stars as Emerson, Lowell, and Longfellow but also to science and scientists. On a rainy night when Rogers gave a lecture on "Physical Forces" some two thousand people showed up. He was an engaging speaker, was respected by the elite, and succeeded in enlisting ardent support of his ideas on education.

For several years Boston had been filling in the Back Bay, in the estuary of the Charles River, to create more land. In 1859 the governor of Massachusetts proposed that some of this land be used for educational purposes. The Society of Natural History and other organizations prepared a petition (of which Rogers was a signer) for the establishment of a Conservatory of Art,

6

Science, and Historical Relics. They envisioned a fanciful building, somewhat like England's famous Crystal Palace, to be erected in the Public Garden, between the Boston Common and the broad, new Commonwealth Avenue. The legislature rejected the petition and the next year turned down another, this one prepared by Rogers and expressing the hope that "public liberality" would also make possible a polytechnic college.

A third petition was then submitted by a committee headed by Rogers. It requested the granting of a block of land in the Back Bay, one-third of it for a Museum of Natural History and two-thirds for the Massachusetts Institute of Technology, which would be comprised of a Society of Arts, a Museum of Arts, and a School of Industrial Science. A report written by Rogers argued that the Institute "would be largely conducive to the progress of the industrial arts and sciences throughout the Commonwealth." The petitioners promised to raise $100,000 for the Institute.

The argument was persuasive. An act chartering M.I.T. and granting the land was passed by the legislature and signed by the governor on April 10, 1861. Fort Sumter fell on April 14 and the threatening storm of the Civil War broke in full fury. "We have nothing doing in science or letters," Rogers

6   Diorama showing the construction of the first M.I.T. building in Back Bay, which was still in the process of being filled in. The finished building of the Boston Society of Natural History (forerunner of the Museum of Science and now housing the Bonwit Teller store) is at the right. In the distance is the wooded Cambridge shore of the Charles River, where M.I.T. is situated today. The diorama was constructed for the New England Life Insurance Company, located on the Boylston Street site of the old M.I.T.

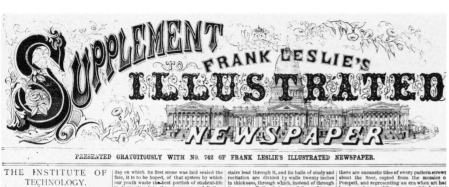

THE INSTITUTE OF TECHNOLOGY.

By Mrs. Harriet Prescott Spofford.

INSTITUTE OF TECHNOLOGY, BOSTON, MASS. SEE PAGE 228.

WILLIAM B. ROGERS, PRESIDENT OF INSTITUTE OF TECHNOLOGY, BOSTON, MASS.—SEE PAGE 228.

7

7   Gushing over the new Institute of Technology, Mrs. Harriet Prescott Spofford wrote: "The day on which the first stone was laid sealed the fate, it is hoped, of that system by which our youth waste the best portion of student-life in burrowing into the grammars and dictionaries of races less enlightened than our own. . . ."

wrote to his brother. "Of course our plans on the Back Bay must wait for the restoration of tranquillity."

The war brought anguish to William Rogers. Though he was born in Philadelphia and was strongly antislavery, he had spent some forty years in Maryland and Virginia and many of his friends were in the South. His brother-in-law, Major James Savage Jr., was wounded, captured, and then died in Charlottesville. His brother Robert, a Union army doctor, lost a hand in a hospital accident. William Rogers gave what support he could on the home front. He was one of the incorporators of the National Academy of Sciences, established to give technical advice to President Lincoln (he later became the academy's president), and he was a founder of the Union Club of Boston.

In spite of the war, planning for M.I.T. proceeded. The incorporators held their first meeting in 1862 and elected Rogers president. The Morrill Act, providing land grants for colleges, was passed by Congress that year. Of the Massachusetts share, three-tenths was allotted to M.I.T., an important financial aid, and the Institute managed to raise the required $100,000 just before the deadline that had been set. Construction of its new home, a neoclassic red brick building with the names of Archimedes and Newton to be chiseled on the frieze, was started in 1863.

After two years the building still was not finished. Impatient, Rogers opened classes on February 20, 1865, at the Mercantile Library in downtown Boston, with studies "suited to the various professions of the Mechanician, the Civil Engineer, the Builder and Architect, the Mining Engineer and the Practical Chemist." He noted in his diary: "Organized the School! Fifteen students entered. May not this prove a memorable day!"

President Rogers taught physics and there were five other members of the faculty. For the term opening the following fall he recruited Charles W. Eliot to join Francis H. Storer, his friend from Harvard days, in teaching chemistry. Eliot had been head of the Chemical Department in the Lawrence Scientific School at Harvard and had attempted to reform the teaching of chemistry there. Bitter when Harvard failed to give him adequate support and passed over him in an appointment to the venerable Rumford Professorship, Eliot had resigned and gone to Europe.

At M.I.T., Eliot and Storer developed a new approach to the teaching of chemistry and wrote a *Manual of Inorganic Chemistry,* which revolutionized the teaching of the subject in America. Eliot's reputation as an educator grew and in 1869, at the age of thirty-four, he was elected president of Harvard — the one who would make a great college into a great university.

Edward C. Pickering, who joined the faculty in its second year, developed a physics teaching laboratory that has long been regarded as the first of its kind. Other colleges had ventured into laboratory instruction and the claim of priority doubtless dangles on a definition. In any case, President Rogers, who had pivoted his educational philosophy on the ancient precept "Learning by Doing," believed that he "was initiating a very important improvement in the methods of scientific training, for which hitherto no provision had been made either abroad or at home."

Pickering not only pioneered in physics education but also in the application of physics to astronomy; he resigned from M.I.T. to become director of the Harvard College Observatory and an eminent astronomer. His brother, William H. Pickering, graduated in 1879 from M.I.T., taught physics there, and then also became a distinguished astronomer at Harvard.

Today it is not easy to appreciate fully the impact that M.I.T. and such innovators as Rogers, Eliot, and the Pickerings had on higher education, which had been stultified by the tradition of the classics and rote learning. In purple prose, a writer for *Frank Leslie's Illustrated Newspaper* in 1869 described the new Institute as "the tomb of the dead languages." It was more than a tomb; it was a source of new ideas and methods, of new vitality.

The burdens of operating M.I.T., especially the fiscal ones, were taxing on President Rogers, whose health had never been rugged. While attending a faculty meeting in 1868 he suffered a slight stroke. His recovery was slow and John D. Runkle, professor of mathematics, was appointed acting president. By 1870 Rogers was still not a well man and he resigned. Runkle became his successor.

8   *Leslie's* pictured a free evening class at M.I.T., sponsored by the Lowell Institute, in which Charles W. Eliot (at left) taught chemistry. "I think the most interesting teaching we did during the first two years," Eliot wrote later, "was to classes of rather middle-aged teachers, both men and women. . . . These men and women, anywhere from twenty-five to fifty-five years of age, were, of course, eager to learn the novel method, but they had not the faintest idea how to learn it, how to work themselves with their own eyes and fingers, to make experiments and to draw their own inferences. We finally had to give them a series of sheets describing the experiments we wanted them to perform, and describing them in a good deal of detail.

"Even then these experienced teachers could not grasp the idea of making their own observations without imitating or copying, then describing accurately what they saw, and lastly, drawing the right inference from what they themselves had done and seen."

A kindly, patriarchal man with a grizzled beard, President Runkle was not as forceful a leader as Rogers but he was popular among the students, who called him "Uncle Johnny," and with most of the faculty.

Among the latter there was an exception, Francis H. Storer, who, when he heard that Runkle was chosen as president, "put on his overcoat and walked out of the school, never to cross the threshold again." He was appointed professor of agricultural chemistry at Harvard and hoped that Harvard would take over M.I.T.

When Storer's partner, Charles W. Eliot, became president of Harvard, Runkle wrote: "It will be a loss to us; but it will also be a gain to have a president of Harvard who believes that the mission of the two institutions is distinct, and that there should be no jealousy or rivalry between them."

Runkle assumed too much. Within months, President Eliot developed a scheme to merge M.I.T. with the ailing Lawrence Scientific School — in fact, as negotiations revealed, to make M.I.T. a part of Harvard.

Though Runkle was a graduate of the Lawrence School, his loyalty was to M.I.T. He was an old friend of Rogers and had shared the dream of developing the Institute. Most members of the M.I.T. Corporation were also loyal and voted down the proposal, one of them referring to the school at Harvard as a "dead carcass." The idea of merger would come up again and again in the next half-century, however.

Independence was sustained through fiscal agonies during Runkle's regime. The Great Boston Fire of 1872 and the Panic of 1873 dealt damaging blows to the Institute's patrons. Tuition had to be doubled to $200, with the result that the student enrollment was halved. The faculty was reduced and so were salaries. M.I.T. professors were making less than Boston school-teachers.

Nevertheless, Tech was a lively place. Charles R. Cross graduated in 1870 and remained as a teacher, assisting Professor Pickering in electrical experiments that would lead to the establishment of the first electrical engineering course in the country a dozen years later. One device they worked on, similar to apparatus developed by Baron von Helmholtz, achieved "electrical transmission of sound." Vibrations of a tuning fork were transmitted through an electromagnet to a tin plate.

Alexander Graham Bell arrived in Boston on April 5, 1871, and on that first day the Scottish immigrant called on his father's friend, Lewis B. Monroe, who was a professor of vocal culture and elocution at M.I.T. With excitement he wrote to his parents in Canada that the Institute had Helmholtz's apparatus and that Monroe had promised to repeat Helmholtz's experiments for him.

As a young voice teacher in London, Bell had been fascinated by Helmholtz's research in acoustics but had lacked the background to understand it. At M.I.T. he received help and in fact did some experimental work in the laboratory there. He heard Cross give Lowell Institute lectures on experi-

2
Precarious Decade

mental mechanics, worked with him on acoustic experiments, and borrowed apparatus for use in his own lecturing.

Bell, who was a professor at Boston University, lectured before the M.I.T. Society of Arts in 1874 on "Visible Speech, or the Science of Universal

9   At the outermost edge of Back Bay when this picture was made in 1872, the new building was an imposing structure. Boylston Street was a muddy road. Presumably one of the four workers was the janitor, whose name might have come right out of Dickens — Darwin C Fogg.

10   Electrical apparatus in the physics laboratory. At right is an electrostatic machine. In the center is what undoubtedly is the Phonautograph, with which Professor Cross and Alexander Graham Bell experimented and which helped lead Bell to the invention of the telephone. One spoke or sang into the cone, causing a diaphragm to vibrate. A bristle attached to the diaphragm scratched a record of the vibrations on a smoked glass, making speech "visible."

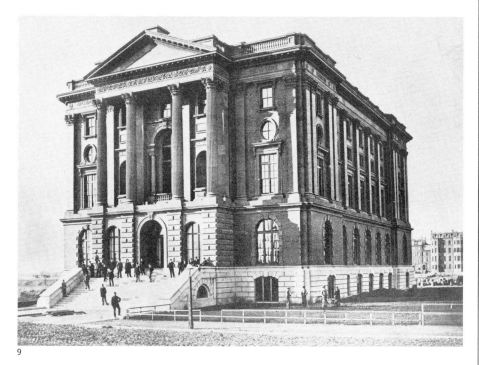

9

10

11

11   Professor John D. Runkle with a mathematics class in 1901, the year before his retirement and death. He had a special interest in astronomy and was associated with *American Ephemeris and Nautical Almanac* for several years.

Alphabetics," and again in 1876, ten weeks after his first, memorable telephoned words to Mr. Watson, on "Telephony or the Telegraphing of Musical Sounds." The latter lecture, he noted, "has at once placed me in a new position in Boston. It has brought me into contact with the best scientific minds of the city." It was the next year that the Bell Telephone Company was organized in Boston.

Apparently Pickering and Cross lacked Bell's vision of the possibilities of telephony, but in later years Bell gave credit for the encouragement and help he received from Cross. Becoming head of the Department of Physics, Cross continued to have a special interest in electrical applications and for a long time was a scientific adviser to the American Telephone & Telegraph Company.

Bell demonstrated his telephone at the great Centennial Exposition in Philadelphia in 1876, but it attracted little attention. M.I.T. had an exhibit at the fair and many of the students and faculty attended, camping on the University of Pennsylvania campus. The exhibition that especially impressed President Runkle demonstrated the Russian system of training engineers through shopwork. Forthwith Runkle established at M.I.T. a School of Mechanic Arts based on the Russian plan, to train industrial technicians. The school provided a pattern for manual training in high schools and state colleges throughout the United States. It also provided shops for regular Institute students. And, worrying about finances, President Runkle wrote to President Emeritus Rogers: "I deeply feel that this step will tide us over these hard times, and put our school on a much broader and firmer foundation."

12

12   William Barton Rogers in his late years, sadly aged.

The foundation was not firm enough, however, and, exhausted by the struggle, Runkle resigned as president in 1878. (He continued to teach mathematics for two more decades.) William Barton Rogers, improved in health though still frail, was asked to return to the presidency. He did so on the condition that $100,000 be raised to assure the Institute's stability and that a search for a successor be started immediately.

The man chosen for president was Francis Amasa Walker, born in Boston and the son of a reform-minded political economist. He had come out of the Civil War a brigadier general, was superintendent of the U.S. Census for 1870 and 1880, and was a professor of political economy at the Sheffield Scientific School at Yale.

General Walker took office in the fall of 1881. There was no inauguration, but special recognition of Rogers was planned for commencement. At graduation exercises, on May 30, 1882, President Walker paid tribute to the seventy-seven-year-old founder and then introduced him to award diplomas. Later he described the farewell of William Barton Rogers:

His voice was at first weak and faltering, but as was his wont, he gathered inspiration from his theme and for the moment his voice rang out in full volume and in those well-remembered and thrilling tones. Then of a sudden, there was a silence in the midst of the speech; that stately figure suddenly drooped, the fire died out of that eye ever so quick to kindle at noble thoughts, and before one of his attentive listeners had time to suspect the cause, he fell to the platform instantly dead.

There was no better demonstration of the effectiveness of the Rogers philosophy of education than the experience of Robert H. Richards, who entered M.I.T. in that first class in 1865.

The son of a prominent family in Maine, young Richards had stumbled through a prep school in England, had failed admission to Harvard, and then had gone to Phillips Exeter Academy where, in spite of working hard, he was at the foot of his class. "I could not adapt to the method of education which revolved around learning dead languages by heart," he later recalled.

Enrolling at M.I.T., Richards discovered:

The method of teaching was new to all of us. We found ourselves bidding goodbye to the old learn-by-heart method, and beginning to study the facts and laws of nature. . . .

I began to see for the first time what school was for, and that it need not worry even the very slow boys. I listened to lectures on chemistry where the lecturer told how things were made, demonstrating the method and providing laboratory work in which I myself handled the apparatus, and my eyes were opened to the wonderful labyrinth ever widening in all directions, of that department of nature. Lectures on physics were accompanied by experiments which happened before my very eyes. . . .

In fact, I found that this new school was teaching me nature, which I had loved and observed all my life; that I was being taught nature by direct contact and that mathematics, languages and history, were nothing but a means to an end.

After graduation, Richards was asked to remain as an instructor in chemistry, and when Francis Storer left in a huff, he suddenly found himself acting head of the department simply because there was no one else to assume the responsibility. Chemistry, by way of qualitative analysis and assaying, led him into mining engineering.

Completion of the transcontinental railroad enabled President Runkle to travel to the West Coast in 1870, to visit mines and smelters en route to arrange such a tour for students and to try to interest affluent mineowners in M.I.T. The next summer he led four professors, including Richards, and twenty-one students on the expedition, which was novel to education. The group collected tons of gold, silver, and other ores in hundred-pound bags for laboratory use at the Institute.

Richards, who for the next thirty years would lead such field trips, proceeded to build much of the equipment needed for processing metals and developed the first laboratories in the world using industrial methods in smelting and refining. The Royal School of Mines in London had a laboratory in which only about an ounce of metal could be processed. Richards did it on a bigger scale. Joseph W. Revere, grandson of Paul Revere and son of the president of Revere Copper Company, had been a student at M.I.T. and helped Richards learn to smelt copper.

3

"What School Was For"

The career of Robert Richards meanwhile had been merging with the career of Ellen H. Swallow, who was M.I.T.'s first coed. The daughter of a farmer-teacher-storekeeper in the Massachusetts hills near the New Hampshire border, she had decided at the age of twenty-six to go to Vassar College, which had opened three years before — the same year that M.I.T. classes started. Through sheer determination and intelligence, for her financial resources were scanty, she earned a degree and resolved to become a chemist.

M.I.T. was the best place for advanced study in chemistry, Miss Swallow found. Thus far it had refused to admit women, though they could attend the Lowell Institute evening classes. Nevertheless, President Runkle agreed to accept her as a special student — without fees, so that she would not be officially enrolled.

At first she was shut in a laboratory like a "dangerous animal," Ellen later recalled, but within a month she was able to record that she was

winning a way which others will keep open.

Perhaps the fact that I am not a Radical or a believer in the all powerful ballot for women to right her wrongs and that I do not scorn womanly duties, but claim it a privilege to clean up and sort of supervise the room and sew things, etc., is winning me stronger allies than anything else. Even Prof. A. accords me his sanction when I sew his papers or tie up a sore finger or

13   In the earliest known photograph of M.I.T. students, Robert H. Richards (with muttonchop whiskers) made a pyramid with Eli Forbes (right) and Whitney Conant, holding the pose for the necessary 11 seconds for a wet plate exposure. The three were ardent and inseparable gymnasts in the three years before their graduation in 1868. Richards was a powerful man, able to lift 600 pounds, and he rowed stroke on the Union Boat Club crew.

14   For thirty years, Professor Richards led a group of students each summer on a field trip to work and study in mines. This picture was made at Capelton, Quebec, in 1888. Presumably the student resting his head on a friend's bosom was clowning — not looking for his mother.

15   Ellen Swallow was serious, rather prim, and very determined as a student.

14

15

dust the table, etc. Last night Prof. B. found me useful to mend his suspenders which had come to grief.

Prof. B. presumably was Bob Richards, three years younger, who became her good friend. In the laboratory one day, after M.I.T. had finally recognized her as a genuine student and given her a degree in 1873, he asked her to be his wife. They were married two years later. She bought boots and a short skirt and they spent their honeymoon on a field trip with Richards's students in Nova Scotia.

For years after that, by buckboard and mule, the Richardses went together on expeditions in mining country. Ellen was the chemist of the team and her competence was recognized when she was elected to the American Institute of Mining Engineers, the first woman member.

But Mrs. Richards had a career of her own. She worked toward an advanced degree but (in the opinion of Richards) the faculty shrank from the idea of giving the Institute's first doctorate to a woman. However she succeeded in opening a Women's Laboratory and was the instructor — without

16   By 1893, Tech had a blast furnace with a water jacket, an improvement over the one which nearly killed Professor Richards and Takuma Dan. Students are shown as they prepare to tap the furnace and draw off the molten metal.

17   Robert H. Richards, then the oldest alumnus, took a turn at bat at the alumni reunion at Nahant in 1909. He was the first president of the Alumni Association, serving from the time of its organization meeting in 1875 until 1880.

16

17

pay — for some seven years until M.I.T. began to admit women as regular students in 1883. The next year she was appointed instructor in sanitary chemistry, a position she held the rest of her life.

A survey of drinking water was undertaken at M.I.T. for the State Board of Health, alarmed at the prevalence of typhoid and other diseases. Mrs. Richards performed thousands of analyses of water to check on contamination by sewage. She analyzed foods for adulterants and textiles and wallpapers for arsenic. She crusaded for better nutrition, better ventilation, better sanitation. The Richards home in Jamaica Plain became a laboratory under a new concept — domestic science.

In fact, Mrs. Richards introduced the word "oekology" in 1892 for the science of "right living." The word failed to catch on as "ecology" did three-quarters of a century later, but another word she coined, "euthenics," is now in the dictionary. The last of several books that she wrote was titled *Euthenics: The Science of Controllable Environment,* a theme for which there would not be substantial public concern for years to come.

Mrs. Richards was a principal organizer of the Home Economics Association — really a founder of the field — and was its first president. She and one of her students, Marion Talbot, held a meeting at M.I.T. in 1881 of college women that led to the formation of the Association of Collegiate Alumnae, now the influential American Association of University Women. Mrs. Richards died in 1911 at the age of sixty-eight, after a heart attack.

18   Schoolmates from the early classes who gathered for the 1909 reunion were, left to right, front row: William Jackson, William E. Stone, and Joseph W. Revere, all of '68; the first man in the rear row has not been identified, but the others are Ernest W. Bowditch '69, Robert H. Richards '68, Charles B. Fillebrown '69, and Eben S. Stevens '68. They spent an afternoon together at Bowditch's estate in Milton.

Professor Richards lived to be one hundred years old. He had become the leading American authority on ore dressing and wrote a definitive, four-volume, 2,800-page work on the subject. He invented various kinds of machinery and was a consultant to such companies as Calumet & Hecla and Anaconda.

In his autobiography, published after he reached ninety, Professor Richards recalled that the most dangerous moment of his career had occurred when he was helping a student with a thesis. The student was Takuma Dan, who at the age of thirteen had been one of fifty-one Japanese children sent to the United States to be educated. After preparation in a Boston school, he entered M.I.T. and was a leading member of the Class of 1878.

For his thesis, Dan chose to smelt iron. Richards, Dan, and other students got the blast furnace in the basement laboratory going furiously and had drawn off a thirty-pound pig when the professor noticed they were all getting sleepy.

"I realized that we were being poisoned by carbon monoxide gas which was leaking out of the porous brick work of the furnace," Richards related. "Fortunately I succeeded in getting all of the students out of the pit and crawling out myself. We all escaped with nothing worse than severe headaches, which wore off in a short time, but we had come as close to a calamity as I ever want to come."

Having survived M.I.T., Takuma Dan returned to Japan, performed effectively as a mining engineer, became director of the Mitsui holding company, Japan's largest cartel, and was the nation's most powerful business leader. He was assassinated in 1932 by a gunman from the Blood Brotherhood for failure to give financial support for aggression in Shanghai.

M.I.T. graduates in mining went into careers throughout the world, but in 1937 the president reported: "Mining Engineering is a field that suffered much during the depression, as was the case with other raw materials industries. The number of students registering in the course was diminished, and our ability to place even the smaller number was impaired." The course was discontinued in 1940. Metallurgy, representing an important new approach to the technology of metals, had taken its place.

4

The Mechs

Mechanical engineering, which was Course I until 1873 (when it switched position with Course II, civil engineering), did not have an auspicious start. The professor was William Watson, fresh from a technical school in Paris, who dressed like a Parisian dandy. The students nicknamed him "Squirty" and made his life miserable. They stacked dripping umbrellas in his tall, pearl-colored beaver hat, glued his favorite blackboard eraser to the desk, and enticed an organ-grinder's monkey into the classroom.

Watson was gone by 1873 and the new professor was Gaetano Lanza, brilliant son of a Sicilian immigrant, who for forty years would be a popular and influential teacher. His textbook on applied mechanics was celebrated in a lugubrious song:

Oh, that wicked old brown book,
That execrable book,
That most infernal book that Getty wrote;
It was tatter'd, it was torn;
'Twas a crime to have it born;
That condemnition book that Getty wrote.

Two years after Getty arrived, Tech acquired its first engine for experimental use, a 16-horsepower steam engine. Lanza was succeeded as head of the department by one of his students, Edward F. Miller '86, and Miller loved steam engines. When M.I.T. moved to Cambridge, Miller filled the lower part of Building 3 (there were great wells from the basement through the

19   Mechanical engineers in the Class of 1876 included Charles T. Main (sitting on a box, third from left), founder of the engineering firm that still bears his name. He served on the Corporation for a total of 25 years and was president of the Alumni Association for 1900–1901. His son, Charles R. Main '09, also became a member of the firm. The others in the picture are Aaron D. Blodgett, Clarence L. Dennet, Francis E. Galloupe, Sumner Hollingsworth, Alfred C. Kilham, Theodore J. Lewis, Edward T. Partridge, and Charles F. Prichard.

20   At about the turn of the century, mechanical engineering students were studying the velocity of a jet in a Harris-Corliss engine with a pitot tube.

21   Professor Lanza was strong in the field of materials testing. This setup was built to test the strength of a brick arch.

22

22   After M.I.T. moved to Cambridge, Building 3 provided plenty of room for the big Steam Laboratory. In the foreground is a Corliss engine.

23   Until the late 1950s, drawing was an important part of the Mechanical Engineering curriculum and in his first semester a student spent six hours a week in the drafting room. The professor here is Arthur L. Townsend '13.

24   In cinematics of a century ago, students learned to represent the movement of machinery in drawing. In kinematic synthesis today they accomplish actual movement in drawing on a computer scope using the KINSYN system developed by Associate Professor Roger E. Kaufman. This KINSYN drawing was made by a graduate student who in a single afternoon developed the linkage of an artificial knee joint that would operate in a natural way, a task that medical researchers have spent years trying to accomplish.

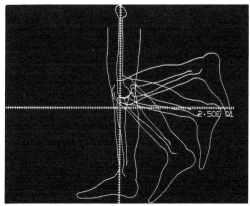

25

25   Professor Samuel C. Collins's invention of the helium cryostat was one of the great accomplishments in Mechanical Engineering. He came to M.I.T. in 1930 as a research associate in physical chemistry and his invention grew out of the low-temperature work in chemistry of Frederick G. Keyes. After years of research, he succeeded in building the first machine in 1946 and thus made possible many advances in cryogenics, such as the production of low-cost liquid oxygen for new steelmaking methods. He was responsible for forming the Cryogenic Laboratory, where still more advanced research is taking place.

second floor) with a wondrous collection of engines, including a giant Corliss, most of them donated by industry. The laboratory was declared to be the finest in the world.

This may have been true but the Corliss was virtually obsolete and many of the other engines soon would be. They were so large and inflexible that they could not be used experimentally. For years students dutifully took readings on their operations and made calculations — not without learning something.

"It was fun," recalls Professor Edward S. Taylor '24, who became a dedicated authority on the internal combustion engine. "You had a form and filled in the numbers. I learned a lot from steam engines, and the machinery was entertaining."

Gradually there were changes in the laboratory to permit teaching fundamental processes such as heat transfer. C. Richard Soderberg '20, head of the department for several years and then dean of engineering, came from steam turbine work at Westinghouse but was enthusiastic about the future of gas turbines and knew that the steam lab had passed its usefulness and was taking up too much valuable room. Joseph H. Keenan '22, who compiled

26 Seven professors who have served as head of the Department of Mechanical Engineering had a dinner reunion in 1974. From the left, they are Jerome C. Hunsaker, 1933–1947; C. Richard Soderberg, 1947–1954; Jacob P. Den Hartog, 1954–1958; Joseph H. Keenan, 1958–1961; H. Guyford Stever, 1961–1965; Ascher H. Shapiro, 1965–1974, and Herbert H. Richardson, who became head in 1974. Dr. Soderberg also was dean of the School of Engineering. Dr. Stever left M.I.T. to become president of Carnegie-Mellon University and later became director of the National Science Foundation.

steam tables used by engineers for the past forty years, certainly was not prejudiced against steam but was very much aware of the laboratory's shortcomings when he became head of the department.

Finally, in 1961, dismantling of the steam lab was accomplished. The walls in Building 3 were floored over and a new Engineering Projects Laboratory, where students could set up a variety of experiments, was installed under the direction of two enterprising young professors, Robert W. Mann '50 and Kenneth R. Wadleigh '43 (later dean for student affairs, and then vice-president, and dean of the Graduate School).

Among other significant educational changes was the elimination of emphasis on graphics. The huge drafting rooms, where students spent tedious hours over drawing boards, were broken up into small classrooms and laboratories. Large-scale testing gave way to strong activity in stress analysis. Ascher H. Shapiro '38, who wrote two classic books on compressible fluid mechanics, was appointed head of the department in 1965 and his field was a dominant one in the department, offering principles that could be applied to many things, from controls to magnetohydrodynamics.

By the end of the decade the educational pendulum had swung and there was increasing activity in applications — in seeking solutions to the problems of transportation, waste disposal, pollution, noise control, power generation. Biomedical engineering was one of the largest areas of research. An M.E. graduate student had a choice of twenty-eight fields, more than in any other department, or could take an interdisciplinary degree in acoustics, biomedical engineering, or environmental studies.

During the early days, civil engineering was the most popular course at M.I.T. It produced more than a third of the graduates in the first decade. America had thousands of miles of railway to build, tunnels to bore, bridges to design, and public works to start. There was a demand for well-trained men.

George F. Swain, who graduated in 1877, became one of the country's most respected civil engineers and was head of the department for twenty-two years. When a railroad bridge in Roslindale collapsed, sending a shocking number of passengers to their death, his analysis of the failure was so authoritative that he was made responsible for the safety of two thousand bridges in Massachusetts. He was chairman of the commission that built the subway in Boston, the first in the United States.

Charles M. Spofford '93, another prominent practicing engineer, was head of the department from 1911 to 1933. Clarence D. Howe '07 taught for a year, then went to the faculty of Dalhousie University, and became one of Canada's greatest statesmen. Roger W. Babson '98 carved a unique career for himself as an entrepreneur and expert on investments. Civil engineering alumni have included other distinguished engineers, railroad executives, and industrialists.

When the nation's first formal program in sanitary engineering was established in 1889, the name of the department was changed to Depart-

5

The Civil Engineers

27 Derby hats were appropriate for young gentleman surveyors to wear when this picture was made at Stony Brook, in the south part of Boston, in the early 1890s.

ment of Civil and Sanitary Engineering. The "Sanitary" was dropped in 1961 in recognition of the comprehensiveness of the department's mission, which now ranged from research and teaching in plastics to hydraulics and soil mechanics. The soil mechanics laboratory, started in the late twenties by Professor Charles Terzaghi, was the first in the country.

For decades, civil engineers were required to learn surveying, and the transit was the symbol of their profession. A stock hero of movie melodrama was the young civil engineer, in boots and open collar, who cut loose the heroine from the path of a locomotive. Gradually glamour was lost to newer engineering fields and in 1961 only a dozen sophomores enrolled in the department.

It was about that time that the digital computer began to have its full impact on the field. Photogrammetry, in which a machine analyzes stereoscopic photographs of a terrain, took the place of much surveying, and Professor Charles L. Miller, who graduated in 1951, devised a way to feed the machine's measurements directly into a computer. The department still has a couple of transits and occasionally students choose to learn surveying, but the computer has become the universal tool, permitting a broad-based systems approach to engineering problems. Student enrollment has nearly doubled in ten years in response to new techniques and challenges in such areas as transportation, environment, and construction.

28   Astronomy and geodesy were taught in civil engineering when in 1901 Professor Alfred E. Burton led a party to Sumatra to observe an eclipse of the sun. Left to right are Gerard H. Mattes '95, assistant hydrographer of the U.S. Geological Survey; Professor Burton; George L. Hosmer '97, instructor in civil engineering; and Harrison W. Smith '97, instructor in physics. Burton also went on an expedition with Robert E. Peary to Greenland, where he made important measurements of glacial movement and temperature. He became the Institute's first dean of students in 1902 and served in that capacity until 1922.

29

29   In 1935, a 115-foot model of the Cape Cod Canal was built in an old hangar for studies to determine the effects in tidal currents, waves, and silting that could be expected from widening and deepening the canal. Shown drained in this picture, a simulation of the bottom of Buzzards Bay appears in the foreground.

30

30   John B. Wilbur '26 developed an intricate Simultaneous Calculator in 1936, with 13,000 parts, including 600 feet of steel tape and nearly a thousand pulleys. It provided in a few seconds a solution of linear algebraic equations to nine or more unknowns. Unfortunately, a long time was required to set up a problem on the machine and the coming of the digital computer made it a museum piece. Professor Wilbur, who was head of the department from 1946 to 1960, wrote words and music for "Arise, Ye Sons of M.I.T.," for many years solemnly sung by students and alumni.

31   Professor Charles L. Miller, shown with students, became the principal protagonist of the computer in civil engineering. A television camera was rigged so that a classroom could get a closeup view of the output. He was head of the department from 1961 to 1969.

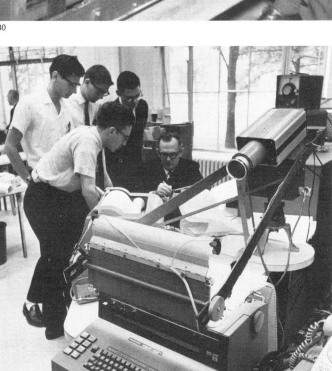

31

"This is a place for men to work, and not for boys to play" is a quotation from President Walker used to characterize not only his administration but the abiding spirit of M.I.T. Actually, the remark was made in a plea for an athletic field and larger gymnasium facilities. The 1880s and 1890s were a time when the image of a student as a mandolin-strumming social lion and athletic hero was established, at M.I.T. as well as at Harvard and Yale. Walker encouraged sports and extracurricular activities.

Sigma Chi, the first fraternity at Tech, was chartered in 1882, the year after Walker became president, and others soon followed. M.I.T. organized a football league with Williams, Amherst, and Tufts in 1886. *The Tech* was started as a student newspaper in 1881. The tradition of freshman-sophomore fights flourished. Samuel C. Prescott '94 had this recollection of President Walker:

One day in the later years of his presidency, hearing unusual commotion in the lobby, he dashed from his office to break up a "rush" which a large group of sophomores had started as a freshman class emerged from a lecture room on the first floor. Without a word, but scarlet with anger, he entered the fray, threw the trouble makers right and left with startling speed, demonstrating with well-directed blows his skill as a trained boxer. In short order, he broke up the fight, and then "with forceful language reminiscent of the army," gave the cowed and surprised students a lesson in college manners which was not soon forgotten.

General Walker was a stalwart man who wore a silk hat, cutaway coat, and striped trousers with military dignity, but he was kindly and had grown up in an atmosphere of social and political reform. As a boy, when his father was teaching at Oberlin College, his tutor was Lucy Stone, whose name became a symbol of women's rights.

Young Walker entered Amherst at fifteen, graduated with high honors and went to war in 1861 as a sergeant major. He was wounded, captured, and sent to Libby Prison, was exchanged, and was brevetted as a general when he had to resign from the Army because of broken health.

Walker's effective direction of the censuses was widely acclaimed and at Yale, where he was appointed in 1873, he produced a whole series of books and papers on such subjects as money, wages, and taxation. He collaborated with Henry Adams in the reform movement, was active in Mugwump politics, and was regarded as a possible member of President Garfield's cabinet.

At M.I.T., President Walker taught political economy to sophomores and for their use completed a textbook he had started at Yale. He converted the course in Science and Literature into one called General Science, with emphasis on economics, political and industrial history, public or business law, and English and modern languages. When cataloguing of the libraries for the first time was completed in 1893, the largest collection was in political economy, thanks to Walker's contributions and interest.

6
A General-Reformer

But Walker strengthened other fields also, inaugurating courses in electrical engineering, chemical engineering, sanitary engineering, geology, and naval architecture. He made a number of brilliant appointments, choosing men who would be leaders in their disciplines and who would shape the growth of departments through the next decades.

32   President Walker kept his office door open and was always accessible to students and faculty. In his time, the Institute had only one telephone and he refused to use it.

33

33   The "New Building" at the corner of Boylston and Clarendon streets, known as the Walker Building after General Walker's death, was completed in 1883. Part of its cost, $165,000, was raised by selling the triangular lot in the center of Copley Square to the city. This picture was made when horsecars were still running on Boylston Street (they made their last trips on Christmas Eve in 1900), and one of them can be seen behind the hacks standing in front of the Buckminster Hotel, which is out of the picture at the right. The Buckminster bar was popularly known to students as "The Chapel" and they were devout in attending services there.

34   The stalwart tug-of-war team of 1892 demonstrated that men could play as well as work.

Student enrollment increased from 302 to 1,011 in President Walker's first ten years. Several new buildings were erected, including a large one at the corner of Clarendon Street, next to the old Rogers Building, which would later be called the Walker Building.

When President Walker arrived, M.I.T. had been in a very precarious state. Now it was beginning to fill out the outlines of the great institution it was destined to become. Its financial problems were not totally solved but it had gained more stability. One step in that direction was to persuade the legislature to give it annual financial support. The effort required to accomplish that, President Walker once remarked, shortened his life by ten years. And on January 5, 1897, when he was fifty-six years old, he died of apoplexy.

The Student

In 1975 the *New York Times* began to worry about reports that "students are engaged in cut-throat competition and all but obsessed with grades." In an editorial titled "The Paper Chase," it observed:

During the rebellious sixties, grades and tests came under heavy fire as the symbols of an allegedly repressive establishment. Although marked by extremism, this anticompetitive movement contained an important ingredient — the search for learning for its own sake. Now, the promise of moderate reforms that might have put education in better focus is being swept away as grades once again establish a "winner takes all" tyranny over education. . . .

The campuses are well rid of the emotional and anti-intellectual hysteria that distorted students' earlier quest for educational reforms. But there must be a middle way of reason.

34

35

36

35 *The Tech* was first published in 1881 and this is a picture of the staff for 1883–1884. Second from the left, sitting on the arm of a chair, is Arthur D. Little '85, a member of the first staff and later editor in chief. His left arm rests on the shoulder of Harry W. Tyler '84, who was then president. The fourth man (in the lower center) is Isaac W. Litchfield '85, also a member of the first staff and president for 1884–1885. Little founded Arthur D. Little, Inc., the first industrial research firm. Tyler served as a professor of mathematics for 46 years and secretary of the faculty for 15. Litchfield served from 1908 to 1917 as editor of *Technology Review*.

36 These were the board members of *The Tech* in 1974–1975, starting at the left and going counterclockwise: Michael D. McNamee '76, editor in chief, Vol. 95; Barb Moore '75, chairperson, Vol. 94; Norman D. Sandler '75, executive editor; Storm Kauffman '75, editor in chief, Vol. 94; Julia Malakie '77, managing editor, Vol. 95; John J. Hanzel '76, chairperson, Vol. 95; Leonard Tower Jr. (right rear), financial consultant; John M. Sallay '78 (with adding machine), business manager; Neal Vitale '75 (with beard, holding broken record), arts editor; Paul E. Schindler Jr. '74 (rear, with beard), contributing editor and editor in chief of Vol. 93; Thomas Klimowicz '77, photo editor, and Mark Suchon '76 (left rear), ad manager.

37

30

39

37   Civil War uniforms and beards were still in style when the cadet officers were photographed in 1869. From the left, they are, front row, Lt. William T. Henry '70; Lt. Carey; Major Channing Whitaker '69 (later mechanical engineering professor); Quartermaster Henry O. Preble '70; Capt. Ernest W. Bowditch '69; Capt. George R. Hardy '70; rear row, Lt. Theodore Tillinghast '70; Lt. Edmund K. Turner '70; Sgt. Mjr. Clark; Adjt. William N. Bannard '70.

38   Cadet artillerymen on Boylston Street in the late 1870s. At the right is Trinity Church, finished in 1877.

39   ROTC leaders in 1974–1975 were, left to right: *front row,* Peter W. Cebelius, company commander, Navy; Catherin H. Osman, midshipman 4/6, Navy; Thomas J. Feeney, cadet S-3, Army; Victor R. Knapp, staff sergeant, Air Force; Martha J. Donahue, squadron commander, Air Force; *rear row,* Jeffrey M. Schweiger, company executive officer, Navy; Nickolas P. Vlannes, major, Air Force; and Dean E. Calcagni, battalion commander, Army.

There is a middle way, and through the years most M.I.T. students have taken it — though unquestionably they have worked harder than the average American college student. Paul E. Schindler Jr. '74, writing in *Technology Review*, said:

It's true that there have been changes. But they have not led to a net loss of education at M.I.T. over the years, as far as I can tell. Instead, the skills necessary to acquire an M.I.T. degree have changed (as skills needed for employment have changed), and in all probability there has been a net increase in the knowledge obtained by each student, both in terms of depth and breadth.

It is also to be remembered that youth is mercurial in temperament, often swinging to extremes in generations or as individuals. To generalize is tricky. Storm Kauffman '75, editor-in-chief of *The Tech,* seeking to classify the student body for incoming freshmen's benefit, explained that "only people from dorms are called nerds, turkeys or freaks and never cretins; and the opposite is true for fraternity members." He made finer distinctions: "Bexley is the home of the Phreak" and "While jocks come from everywhere, only Jocks come from fraternities."

40   M.I.T. students have always enjoyed elaborate pranks. In 1926 a car was hauled to the East Campus dormitory roof.

41   In 1927, fun-loving Sigma Chis had a Black Maria as a chapter bus.

42   In the fall of 1949 the Harvard Bridge was closed for repairs. In advance of the formal reopening students staged their own ceremony, renaming it Technology Bridge.

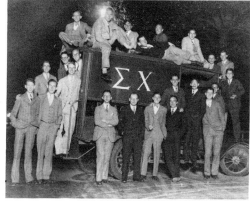

41

42

40

All said in good fun, of course. And one generalization that can be made is that all kinds of people have attended M.I.T., they have learned all kinds of things, and they have had all kinds of fun. But certainly their "look" has changed.

43 The date of this ball hasn't been pinned down, but obviously it was Halloween in the time of conga lines and jitterbugging.

44 The M.I.T. campus has cosmopolitan look, for 18 percent of the students are foreigners.

44

43

7

A Matter of Chemistry

Looking back fifty years to the M.I.T. he knew as a student (1894–1898), Roger W. Babson was dismayed that his professors had failed to anticipate the automobile, airplane, photography, and motion picture industries. He wrote: "The leading technical institute in America was content to teach railroading, electrical engineering, theoretical chemistry, and other well developed subjects."

Although Babson demonstrated business acumen, he could be very wrong about some things. (He went to his grave convinced that an "antigravity insulator" could be found.) Although M.I.T. was less a center for innovation in the nineties than in later years — when it has been far out front in creating new technologies — it was educating students who would be innovators. And at that very time, the Institute was moving to a new level of scholarly research, particularly in what Babson called "theoretical chemistry."

The outstanding chemist was James Mason Crafts, who was internationally prominent. A dignified man with formidable sidewhiskers, he had studied at Heidelberg and Freiberg and had spent seventeen years in Paris in research on organic synthesis. The Friedel-Crafts Reaction, a product of that period, is still employed.

Among his students at M.I.T., Crafts was notorious for using German textbooks in his classes and for rapidly erasing with his left hand the equations he was putting on the blackboard with his right hand.

45 Chemistry students in the Class of 1890. At the extreme left is Pierre S. du Pont, who with his cousins, T. Coleman du Pont '84 and Alfred I. du Pont '86, assumed control of E. I. du Pont de Nemours & Company and made it a modern corporate giant. He was president from 1915 to 1919. More than a score of du Ponts have attended M.I.T. Another chemist in the Class of 1890 was Willis R. Whitney, probably the spectacled student in the deep center. He became the first director of the Research Laboratory of the General Electric Company and was regarded as the dean of industrial research. Others in the above picture are Frederick E. Harnden, S. B. Sheldon, Graham Robinson, Willard C. Tillson, Edmund T. Simpson, Wallace Macgregor, Henry H. Pope, Charles E. Martin, Louis Schmidt, James A. Carney, Herbert C. Tuttle, George E. Merrick, H. B. Taylor, William H. Collins, Frank W. Atwood, and George W. Fuller.

46

47

48

46   James Mason Crafts, who headed M.I.T. for more than three years, first as chairman of the faculty and then as president. A graduate of Harvard, he joined the M.I.T. chemistry faculty in 1870.

47   William D. Coolidge '96, who succeeded Willis R. Whitney as director of the Laboratory of Physical Chemistry at M.I.T. and then as director of the General Electric Research Laboratory. Whitney improved the efficiency of electric lamps by developing a new kind of carbon filament and then Coolidge, directing the research of a score of chemists for four years, developed the ductile tungsten filament which was far better. He died in 1975 at the age of 101.

48   Robert B. Woodward '36, Donner Professor of Chemistry at Harvard, who synthesized quinine and other compounds and received the Nobel Prize in Chemistry in 1965.

After President Walker's death, Crafts was elected chairman of the faculty to carry on administrative functions and in the fall of 1897 he was named president. Three years of administration proved as much as he desired and he resigned at the end of 1899 to return to research.

Crafts "fostered a spirit of cooperation between the professor and the advanced student, and foresaw the development at the Institute of a graduate school devoted to research in pure science," according to chemistry's historian, Tenney L. Davis '13. And the roles of research in education and of education in research at M.I.T. cannot be overemphasized.

This development was carried further by Professor Arthur A. Noyes '86, who organized the Research Laboratory of Physical Chemistry in 1903 (personally contributing $3,000 a year for its support). The laboratory was renowned for the excellence of its work. The first three doctorates awarded by M.I.T. were given in 1907 to students of Professor Noyes who had done research there.

Willis R. Whitney '90, who was associated with Noyes in the laboratory, left to be the first director of the great Research Laboratory of General Electric Company. William D. Coolidge '96, who succeeded Noyes as director of the Laboratory of Physical Chemistry, later succeeded Whitney as director of the General Electric Laboratory. Noyes initiated a *Review of American Chemical Research* which became the indispensable *Chemical Abstracts* of the American Chemical Society.

49   Robert S. Mulliken '17, who as Distinguished Service Professor of Physics and Chemistry at the University of Chicago was awarded the Nobel Prize in Chemistry in 1966.

50   Avery A. Ashdown '24, a devoted teacher of chemistry and friend of thousands of students. The graduate residence (behind him) was named Ashdown House in his honor.

51   Jennifer Makowski, a graduate student from the University of Edinburgh, and Charles A. Mims, a postdoctoral from Berkeley, at work with a molecular beam–scattering apparatus in a laboratory under the direction of John Ross '51.

50

49

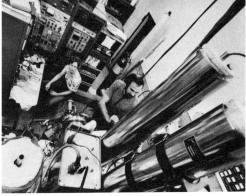

51

52

52   The Camille Edouard Dreyfus Building for Chemistry in McDermott Court. Like the Green Building in the background, it was designed by I. M. Pei ('40) & Partners.

Noyes and Samuel P. Mulliken '87 pioneered in the systematic identification of organic compounds. Mulliken's son, Robert S. Mulliken, who graduated in chemistry in 1917, would become a University of Chicago professor and win a Nobel Prize in 1966.

Eminent chemists in Noyes's time included Henry Paul Talbot '85, who became head of the department in 1901 and developed a procedure by which minute quantities of rare elements could be detected. Frederick G. Keyes, who headed the department for many years, conducted low-temperature research that laid the foundation for cryogenics. Arthur C. Cope, who became head in 1944, revealed transannular reactions, an unexpected phenomenon in organic chemistry. Richard C. Lord, now director of the Spectroscopy Laboratory, pioneered in infrared absorption techniques. John C. Sheehan achieved the first synthesis of penicillin. Through the years there has been a long line of first-rate chemists, such as Walter C. Schumb, George Scatchard, James F. Norris, James A. Beattie, and Leicester F. Hamilton '14, who have made important contributions, not the least of which has been the education of students. John Ross '51 and then Glenn A. Berchtold followed Cope in heading the department.

Dropping of the chemistry requirement for all M.I.T. students in the sixties and of the laboratory requirement for introductory chemistry put an end to most of the vast, dreary, smelly undergraduate laboratories. Construction of the handsome Camille Dreyfus Building in 1969, with bright, efficient labs, ended the crowded conditions in which graduate students had to work in shifts.

On October 24, 1900, a new president was inaugurated: Henry Smith Pritchett, an astronomer with a neatly clipped beard. For three years he had been superintendent of the U.S. Coast and Geodetic Survey. He was responsible for reorganizing the Office of Standard Weights and Measures as the science-oriented Bureau of Standards. He had a reputation for being a strong administrator.

Just three weeks later President Pritchett was introduced to the Cane Rush and to a tragedy.

The Cane Rush was a ritualized scrap between freshmen and sophomores which had started back in the eighties. The strongest men in the freshman class held the cane, a four-foot stick with a knob at each end, and as many as 150 classmates formed around them in defensive circles. The sophomores, in two flying wedges, attacked in an attempt to seize the cane.

At the end of fifteen minutes in the 1900 event, a pistol was fired to end the struggle. There were nineteen sophomore hands and eleven freshman hands on the cane. Two freshmen were unconscious and another, Hugh C. Moore, stalwart center of the football team, was dead with a dislocated neck.

In a sorrowing statement, President Pritchett declared the Cane Rush must never be held again. Furthermore, he said: "Plans have been for some time under consideration in the Institute for the establishment of a system of physical culture which should assist in upbuilding of the health of the general body of students rather than in the development of expensive and time-consuming athletic contests."

8
A Rough Beginning

THE BOSTON GLOBE—FRIDAY, NOVEMBER 16, 1900.

THE FATAL CANE RUSH ON THE SOUTH END GROUNDS.

53   A *Boston Globe* artist pictured the 1900 Cane Rush as a donnybrook; the reality must have been worse.

54

55

54   Football survived many years in the annual freshman-sophomore Field Day game, which was rough. Some players wore helmets, noseguards, or shinguards and some did not.

55   This was how Technology Field looked on Field Day, date undetermined. The chara-banc's banner proclaimed NOT SOUSED, WE'RE HAPPY.

What Pritchett had in mind became apparent later. In the fall of the next year, the Cane Rush was replaced by Field Day, with three freshman-sophomore contests: a football game, a tug-of-war, and a relay race. A week before the event, the president called a student mass meeting, of which *The Tech* reported as follows:

Having finished his remarks in regard to the abolition of the Cane Rush, the President spoke of Football at the Institute. The purport of his remarks was that he was not in favor of football at Tech because very few men could afford the time for the game. After further remarks, the President left the hall and many students thinking the meeting adjourned, left at the same time, so that when action was taken in regard to football, there were about half the original number of students present. The Chairman, after a few remarks, asked for an expression from those who wished to have Technology represented by a football eleven. The resulting vote was 119 against to 117 in favor. On the strength of this opinion from a small minority, the team, to the surprise of all, was disbanded.

The decision, though it appeared to have been shrewdly engineered, was one of the most important ones ever made at M.I.T., since it saved the Institute from the evils of big-time football and strengthened the philosophy of athletics for fun. Football was becoming frighteningly brutal (there were eighteen fatalities in 1905) and the era of big stadium spectacles was about to begin.

M.I.T. had been using various fields for sports and now acquired its own, Technology Field, in Brookline. The Class of 1881 erected a gate on which were inscribed the lines of F. Gelett Burgess '87:

Not the quarry, but the chase,
Not the laurel, but the race,
Not the hazard, but the play,
Make me, Lord, enjoy alway!

Field Day would go through many changes. In 1927, Ralph T. Jope, president of the Class of 1928 and chairman of the Institute Council, introduced the glove fight, a popular event at an Ohio college. Freshmen wore white gloves on their left hands and sophomores wore red ones on the right, and each tried to capture the others' gloves.

In the fall of 1968 the sophomores were beginning to prefer antagonists other than freshmen. Steve Ehrmann, president of the Class of 1971, explained, "Field Day is becoming less relevant to M.I.T. life," and the sophomores voted to boycott it. There have been no Field Days since.

President Pritchett may have been somewhat high-handed in disposing of football, but apparently there was no resolute opposition. He was interested in the improvement of the student's lot. He built a new gymnasium and established the Tech Union, where the students could eat and drink. He had studied for his doctorate at Munich and he favored the German tradition of conviviality, encouraging the "Tech Kommers" on Saturday nights where the boys could get together over beer and sandwiches and sing.

Boston clergymen protested against the beer, but Pritchett stood his ground, arguing that only a half-pint per student was consumed during "discussion of topics of technical and general interest, in buildings under my control."

Pritchett did not come out so well on another issue. President Eliot of Harvard had written him a letter of welcome, giving assurance that the Lawrence Scientific School and M.I.T. "can prosper abundantly side by side in hearty cooperation."

Harvard had made another proposal for union while Crafts was president, the M.I.T. Corporation had turned it down, and the question seemed to be settled. But in 1903, Gordon McKay, an inventor of shoe machinery, left a large bequest to Harvard for applied science. Harvard now had the prospect of millions for its Lawrence School. And M.I.T., stifling for lack of resources and space to grow, had the prospect of increased competition from a vitalized school at Harvard.

Early in 1904 Boston newspapers disclosed that Harvard and Tech were negotiating again. Not only disclosed it, but kept up a din to which the voices of angry M.I.T. alumni were added.

It happened that Tech was planning its first big alumni reunion for June of that year and, while President Pritchett conducted the delicate negotiations with Harvard, the assembly of alumni for a joyous reunion began to acquire undertones of mobilization for rebellion. There was reason for concern. A pro-merger group, including Andrew Carnegie, had gone so far as to buy a tract of land (where the Harvard Business School now stands) as the site for M.I.T. when it should come under the wing of Harvard.

There was indeed joy among the 1,600 alumni who attended the reunion, but indignation about merger with Harvard kept showing through. At the first big event, Tech Night at Boston Pops, F. Gelett Burgess, the wag from the Class of 1887, supplied new words for "John Brown's Body" that were sung loudly by roistering alumni:

You can't make crimson out of cardinal and gray . . .
   As Tech goes marching on.
We don't give a damn for Ha-a-vud . . .
   As Tech goes marching on.

The next day the alumni went by steamboat to Nantasket, marched on the beach, and performed stunts on the lawn of the Atlantic House. The Class

9

The Reluctant Bride

56   President Henry S. Pritchett with his daughter, Edith, who was born in 1904.

of 1876 seemed to express the prevailing sentiment about merger, parading with a banner proclaiming SPIRIT OF '76 — INDEPENDENCE.

Back at the Hotel Somerset that night for a dinner, the alumni were in gay spirits but the time had come to face the issue. President Pritchett spoke soothingly and promised that no decision would be made without consultation with alumni and faculty. One of his strongest arguments for ties with Harvard had to do with an educational question that underlay Tech's founding and would be of deep concern for years to come: Can an undergraduate be educated as a professional? President Rogers thought he could.

President Pritchett now asserted: "Everything points to the fact that we are in a transition stage, and that a new step must soon be taken in this country in technical education: either the courses must be lengthened or some of the strongest schools become graduate schools, or some other means must be taken to meet the changing demands for education and for research in technical schools. But any one of these changes means the addition of great cost."

Other speakers challenged the president's point of view. Dean Alfred E. Burton, to frequent applause, declared: "I welcome competition. . . . The Institute of Technology is an undergraduate college. . . . Why let us talk just now of the advanced graduate work as being of more importance? . . .

57   Members of the Class of 1876, parading at the alumni outing at Nantasket in 1904, expressed their opinion about merger with Harvard.

58   F. Gelett Burgess '87 caricatured himself in *The Purple Cow and Other Nonsense.* After graduating from M.I.T., he became an instructor in topological drawing at the University of California. He was one of the founders of *The Lark,* a bohemian magazine in San Francisco, and "The Purple Cow" appeared in its first issue.

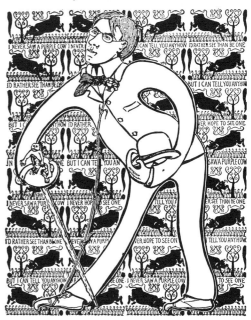

Ah, Yes! I Wrote the "Purple Cow" —
I'm Sorry, now, I Wrote it!

But I can Tell you Anyhow,
I'll Kill you if you Quote it!

59

59   Andrew Carnegie and Henry Pritchett when the latter was president of the Carnegie Foundation for the Advancement of Teaching.

We don't want to try the experiment at once of having an organization which takes on one side of the river the undergraduate and the other side of the river the graduate. Nor do we want to have all the engineering work on one side of the river and the research on the other. . . . President Eliot has told us that his idea is that our relation should be something like that of Radcliffe. This simply means a sort of annex."

James Phinney Munroe, editor of *The Technology Review,* pulled out all the stops. He recalled his own graduation day in 1882, when William Barton Rogers dropped dead on the platform — "killed by his devotion to the Institute." He described the funeral of President Walker, "gone because he had worn himself out in building up, from those early days of abject poverty, the Institute of Technology, so that he left it comparatively rich in money, infinitely rich in reputation, and, as I have said, left it the greatest technological institute in the world. . . . If we do not hand on that trust undiminished, untarnished, then I say we are traitors to those men and to the Institute. [Tremendous applause and cheers.]"

President Pritchett persevered in working out a plan by which M.I.T. would keep its name but move to the site near Harvard and become Harvard's engineering school. The faculty voted against the plan, 56 to 7. Alumni voted against it, 2,035 to 834. The Corporation nevertheless voted in 1905 to go ahead with the merger — on condition that M.I.T. could sell its Copley Square properties to pay for new buildings. But within a few months the Supreme Judicial Court held that the Institute could not sell the land. So M.I.T. had no dowry and the marriage with Harvard was called off.

The episode was hardly one to strengthen Pritchett's position as president. He had become a friend of Andrew Carnegie and had been discussing with him the plight of underpaid professors. The philanthropist decided to establish the Carnegie Foundation for the Advancement of Teaching with an endowment of $10,000,000 and asked Pritchett to be its president. At the end of 1905 Pritchett resigned from M.I.T.

Pritchett had been serving as head of a commission which managed, in spite of bitter opposition from the Late George Apley and other Bostonians who were fond of the mud flats, to dam the Charles River and create the Basin, which (although he couldn't have foreseen it) would enhance the Institute's water view in the future. His biographer, Abraham Flexner, comments: "To nothing that he achieved during his brief residence in Boston did Pritchett look back in subsequent years with greater pride and satisfaction."

10

The Scot from New Zealand

After his resignation, Pritchett agreed to spend half-time at Tech for another year. Professor Noyes was elected chairman of the faculty and doubtless could have been president had he been willing. He became acting president in 1907 and served until Richard Cockburn Maclaurin was inaugurated in 1909.

Maclaurin was so exactly suited to the task at M.I.T. and he came in such a roundabout way that his choice surely would have confirmed his Scottish forebears' belief in predestination. He was born near Edinburgh and when he was four years old his father, a United Presbyterian minister, took the family to New Zealand and rode circuit on the Maori frontier as a missionary. The father was well educated and the son was studious. After taking a degree in mathematics at University College in Auckland he went to Cambridge University where he distinguished himself and, in seven years, qualified for degrees in mathematical physics and law. He returned to New Zealand to teach law and to become dean of the law school, at Victoria University College. He did not lose interest in science, however, and began to work on a book on the physics of light.

Columbia University was looking for an exceptional mathematical physicist and Maclaurin was recommended. He accepted the invitation and arrived in New York in 1908, planning to finish the book and teach physics indefinitely. One of the first friends he made was George V. Wendell, who graduated from M.I.T. in 1892 and taught physics there for fifteen years before resigning in 1907 to become head of the department at Stevens Institute of Technology. Wendell decided Maclaurin would make an ideal president of M.I.T. and arranged to take him to Boston for a visit to the Institute and a talk with Acting President Noyes. (Independently, Professor Michael Pupin of Columbia also recommended Maclaurin to the Executive Committee.)

Other interviews followed and in November, less than a year after he arrived in the United States, Maclaurin was elected by the M.I.T. Corporation.

A second All-Technology reunion had already been planned for June of 1909 and this made a perfect occasion for the inauguration of Maclaurin. For three days alumni celebrated, breaking into roaring class and Tech yells at the slightest excuse. They took over Symphony Hall for the Pops, for the inauguration, for commencement, and for a gala dinner. They went by steamboat to Nahant for Class Day and the next day to Nantasket to march on the beach and to have stunts. Eben S. Draper of the Class of 1878 was governor of Massachusetts and held a glittering reception at the State House.

President Maclaurin did not fail to challenge the alumni at this time of clamorous enthusiasm. M.I.T. would have to find a new site, the money to pay for it, and the money for new buildings. "This institution is certainly not going backward," he declared at the dinner. "It has become a national asset, and it is going to continue to be a great national asset and a greater one."

On a visit to Boston in April, Maclaurin and his wife had been guests of Charles A. Stone '88 at his home on the water side of Beacon Street. Looking across the new Charles River Basin at the desolate expanse of filled land on the Cambridge shore, Maclaurin asked, "Why isn't that a good site for Technology?"

Stone explained that opposition from Harvard would make such a location impossible. Because of its tax-exempt holdings in Cambridge, Harvard was already vulnerable to municipal opposition, and the presence of another tax-exempt institution in the city would intensify its problem. Furthermore, wealthy Harvard alumni who were prospective donors for Tech would be opposed.

But Maclaurin didn't give up the idea. On the day before his inauguration he walked across the bridge for a closer look at the land. After further discussion, Everett Morss '85, who was president of Simplex Wire and Cable Company in Cambridge, approached the principal owner of the land and determined that it could be purchased. Maclaurin then broached the matter to President A. Lawrence Lowell of Harvard (which had just given him an honorary degree). Lowell's response was that the choice of a Cambridge site would "not improbably imperil the financial stability of both institutions."

Another possible site was a tract of thirty-five acres in the triangle along Commonwealth Avenue in Boston, west of what is now the Boston University Bridge. Maclaurin discussed it with T. Coleman du Pont '84, president of E. I. du Pont de Nemours and Company.

Du Pont thought this tract was not big enough. "Almost invariably," he said, "when a man comes to me to approve plans for a new factory, I tell him to double the size of everything, and almost invariably I wish afterward that I had used a larger factor of safety. Technology will occupy a great position in the future and must have room to grow." He pledged $500,000

60   When he was elected president of M.I.T., Richard C. Maclaurin had a luxuriant moustache in the current British style.

61

on condition that the site be increased to forty-five acres and that $1,500,000 additional be raised from others.

At about this time, Springfield alumni offered a free site of thirty acres if the Institute would move there. Then Cambridge was heard from. Four civic associations urged that it come to Cambridge and the City Council passed a resolution favoring such a move.

In October of 1911, President Maclaurin boldly announced that construction of a new building would start the following spring. Owners of

62

the Cambridge land had agreed to sell forty-six acres for $775,000. Du Pont's pledge, plus gifts and bequests (including one from Mrs. Emma Rogers, widow of the founder), provided the money.

The president still did not know where funds for the building could be found. Early in 1912, Frank W. Lovejoy '94, general manager of Eastman Kodak Company, wrote that George Eastman, president, "would be inclined to help out." Maclaurin arranged to meet Eastman in New York and described M.I.T.'s potential. Maclaurin was about to leave the meeting when Eastman suddenly asked:

"What will it cost to put up the new building?"

"Two and a half millions," Maclaurin replied.

"I will send you a draft."

Planning the new M.I.T. was an enormous undertaking. John R. Freeman '76, internationally prominent engineer from Providence, Rhode Island, and a member of the Corporation, had been developing preliminary specifications and he spared no effort in investigating new methods of construction, ventilation, and lighting. Faculty members submitted elaborate studies of their laboratory and classroom needs. From twenty-five other universities 2,061 photostats of blueprints for existing facilities were collected.

Freeman proposed "architectural details and outlines derived from the Greek Classic style, which have satisfied the human eye for 2,000 years, modifying the windows as needed for science study as contrasted with the dim religious light of a temple." He wanted a unified building, "avoiding to the maximum extent the need for men racing across lots, often scantily clad, from one building to another in Boston's raw climate."

The space needed was a million square feet, and how to get that without making the building look like a factory was a problem. Professor Constant Désiré Despradelle gave special attention to that aspect.

Despradelle was a flamboyant Frenchman with a great black beard who had joined the architecture faculty in 1893. He provided the basic ideas for the design of the new Boston Museum of Fine Arts. He made drawings with elaborate architectural refinements of the basic plan for the new Tech, as did another professor, C. Howard Walker '99. Despradelle died in 1912, just four months after he had been made head of the Department of Architecture.

Construction of the new building could not start in 1912 as President Maclaurin had hoped. One delaying problem was that of selling the campus

11

Bosworth's Building

63   John R. Freeman's concept of the new building, drawn by Harold E. Kebbon, the resident architect. Freeman suggested that the old Rogers Building be moved to Cambridge.

STUDY·NO·7
NOT·FINAL·

64

65

in Boston, which M.I.T. hoped would yield $3,000,000. There were legal complications and a decision was made to leave the Department of Architecture in the old Rogers Building.

In early 1913, W. Welles Bosworth '89 was chosen as the architect and those partners of the Class of 1888, Charles A. Stone and Edwin S. Webster, as the engineers. Webster had been president of the Alumni Association in 1909 and Stone would be president in 1916.

The engineering problems were formidable. The land was made from mud pumped from the Charles River and earth from subway construction. A total of 22,000 piles had to be driven.

64   One of Désiré Despradelle's drawings envisioned a large plaza in front of the central building and an "Experimental Court" behind it.

65   This is one of Welles W. Bosworth's studies, showing complete serenity, perfect symmetry, and a 50-foot Minerva.

66

67

66 Gathered to see the cornerstone trucked to Cambridge are, left to right: President Maclaurin; Everett Morss '85, a leading alumnus; Harold E. Kebbon, resident architect; Allyne L. Merrill '85, secretary of the faculty; Alfred E. Burton, dean of students; J. R. Lotz of the Bosworth staff; Welles W. Bosworth; Walter Humphreys '97, then registrar; Albert S. Smith, superintendent of buildings and power; and Horace S. Ford, who had just started his 20 years as bursar, to be followed by 16 as treasurer. At the far left is M. R. Kinsella, the driver.

67 Erection of the Great Dome was a major engineering undertaking, requiring elaborate forms for the concrete. It was patterned after the Pantheon dome, which is 42 feet wider.

Bosworth accepted the basic plan, but whereas early drawings had tended to make the building look like the Parthenon, he found his inspiration in Thomas Jefferson's University of Virginia, with its Pantheon dome as the central feature. He took Maclaurin and Stone to Charlottesville to convince them of the rightness of his judgment. He chose Indiana limestone for the facade and, although at one point, when the financial pinch was acute, the substitution of brick was proposed, Bosworth prevailed.

The dome was planned as the cap for a large, circular auditorium and when the auditorium had to be canceled to cut costs elimination of the dome was proposed. Bosworth protested that the straight lines of the building "must be made to lead to a climax, or focal point, at the top," and he solved the problem by placing the library under the dome.

Bosworth was so pleased with the M.I.T. building that he built a miniature replica of it as his home near Paris. But he was always sad that no sculptor was commissioned to do a fifty-foot statue of Minerva for the Great Court as he had suggested. Not long before his death in 1966 at the age of ninety-seven he was still urging that such a sculpture be installed.

68   M.I.T. in March 1929. The Daniel Guggenheim Aeronautical Laboratory, the Pratt School of Naval Architecture, and the first of the two parallel East Campus dormitories had been built in the twenties.

From the perspective of nearly half a century, Eero Saarinen, whose Kresge Auditorium and Chapel are monuments of his creativity, wrote this appraisal of Bosworth's buildings:

These were the buildings that we all disliked in the thirties and forties because of their pseudo-classical sterility. But let us not dismiss them so easily just because we once disliked them. One can see that they form a unity: they create an environment. They have also proven quite useful. They were built in parts and X-number of units was added. They were built on the principle of continuous space. Fortunately Welles Bosworth chose a bay which has proven very workable despite hundreds of shifts and alterations within. It is possible that had the buildings been done on a complete modular system with movable partitions they would have proven less flexible. Parenthetically, the Bosworth M.I.T. buildings have been called dull and monotonous, but I have come to the point where I welcome more dullness and more monotony in our cityscapes instead of all the visual clashes typical of our time. . . . Specialized space (auditoriums, etc.) is different; but it seems to me that for academic instruction, space such as that in the old M.I.T. buildings provides an excellent example of what in the long run proves to be economical space.

That is one modern architect's opinion. To the public, and to its own community, the buildings have become a symbol of the grandeur of M.I.T.'s aspiration, the stateliness of its intellectual tradition, the austerity of scientific thought.

The completion of the new building was the occasion for a celebration in 1916 that has never been matched at M.I.T.

New York alumni set the pace when, five hundred–strong, they arrived on the S.S. *Bunker Hill* on June 12. They were greeted by a twenty-one-gun salute and a special issue of *The Tech* filled with news of their trip wirelessed from the ship during the night. They marched to Copley Square behind the M.I.T. battalion band to join other alumni who had come from all parts of the world.

There was a farewell ceremony at the old Rogers Building and then a laying of the cornerstone for Walker Memorial, a building for which alumni had been raising money ever since the death of President Walker.

The last commencement in the Rogers Building was held the next morning and then the alumni were transported on three steamboats to Nantasket for an outing. There was a fancy dress parade on the beach, led by the New Hampshire delegation with a huge papier-mâché beaver, Tech's official mascot. Professor Richards was at the head of a group of alumni from the first five years, hobbling on canes and crutches which they suddenly dropped to start skipping ropes. Godfrey L. Cabot '81, Boston's great aviation enthusiast, buzzed the crowd in a "monster" hydroplane and formed his class numerals in the sky.

12

A Time to Rejoice

69

69   President Maclaurin and Charles A. Stone, president of the Alumni Association, doffed their silk hats and shook hands at the laying of the cornerstone for Walker Memorial in 1916.

70   Franklin D. Roosevelt, assistant secretary of the Navy, reviewed a power squadron on the Charles River. Designed by alumni as submarine chasers in anticipation of the U.S. entrance into the war, the boats joined the flotilla for the reunion. At right is Edwin S. Webster.

71   Corporate affiliations were well represented in the Nantasket parade by such names as Coca-Cola, Karo, and Domino. At the upper right is the Atlantic Hotel.

72   This is the famous Bucentaur used for the ceremonial crossing of the Charles River. A hawser had damaged the plaster on the port bow.

70

71

72

The crowd returned in time to gather at the new building in Cambridge at dusk, an estimated ten thousand filling banked seats at the sides of the Great Court. Starting at the Rogers Building, robed faculty and Corporation members bore a chest containing the Institute's seal to the Bucentaur, an elaborate replica of a Venetian state barge, and were rowed across the river. They landed amid the glare of rockets and searchlights and carried the chest to the new building.

Then Professor Ralph Adams Cram of the Department of Architecture presented a pageant, "Masque of Power," which he had written and over which he presided as Merlin. Pageants were popular spectacles in those days and the word "corny" had not yet been invented. This one told about man's conquest of Nature and his confrontation with Greed, Vainglory, Selfishness, and War and how "finally appears Merlin, the Master, before the throne of Alma Mater, to lead before her the forces of civilization who in her name have conquered Nature."

The formal dedication of the new building was held in the Great Court the next afternoon following an impressive academic procession. In his speech, President Maclaurin said of the still-anonymous Eastman gift that "it will have far-reaching consequences for the country at large, for its aim is to strengthen American industry at the base by fixing it firmly on the solid rock of science."

73   Ralph Adams Cram, professor of architecture, represented Merlin (magic-making technology) in the pageant that he wrote for the reunion.

74   A not-very-ferocious squad presented a "Pyrrhic Dance of Gladiators" in the pageant.

73

74

75

76

The orator of the day, Senator Henry Cabot Lodge, went about as far as a Harvard-bred politician could go when he asserted that M.I.T. "has risen so high in its chosen field that no one can attribute to parochial pride the declaration that it stands second to none in the world."

That night alumni gathered at Symphony Hall for a white-tie dinner. Speakers included Orville Wright, Alexander Graham Bell, and Michael I. Pupin. Still trying to meet the Institute's financial commitment, which by now totaled $7,000,000, President Maclaurin announced that nine alumni had given a million, of which $800,000 came from T. Coleman '84, Pierre '90, Irenée '97, and Lammot du Pont '01. He disclosed that "Mr. Smith" was offering $5 for each $3 contributed by others, bringing the total raised to $3,150,000. (The full goal was reached by the end of the year.)

In a remarkable technological accomplishment for that time, Symphony Hall had been linked by Bell's telephone with thirty-four cities in which alumni were gathered, and the evening ended when all, from coast to coast, sang "The Star-Spangled Banner."

75   T. Coleman du Pont, chief marshal, assembled the principals for the dedication of the new building. He faces, from left to right, Senator Henry Cabot Lodge, Governor Samuel W. McCall, and President Maclaurin.

76   A bust of William Barton Rogers was displayed under a big picture of the old Rogers Building at the banquet in Symphony Hall winding up the 1916 celebration.

The establishment of M.I.T. in Cambridge was President Maclaurin's most spectacular accomplishment but there were other advances — new programs, such as one in aeronautics, a new emphasis on research, and a strengthening of the faculty. And finally what appeared to be a workable agreement with Harvard was achieved in 1913.

Under this plan, Harvard would supply fifteen professors and $100,000 a year, chiefly from the McKay fund, for joint courses at M.I.T. in civil and sanitary engineering, mechanical engineering, electrical engineering, and mining and metallurgy. This would require more room than was planned for the new building, so Coleman and Pierre du Pont and Charles Hayden '90 provided $215,000 for an additional wing to house mining.

Harvard had not, however, consulted trustees of the McKay fund about the plan and within three months they asked for a judicial determination whether the arrangement with M.I.T. violated terms of the bequest. The legal process promised to be a long one.

Nevertheless the two institutions decided to go ahead with the joint experiment. Students enrolling in the fall of 1914 could qualify in the four fields for degrees from both M.I.T. and Harvard. During the next four years some three hundred students earned joint bachelor's degrees and fifty, advanced degrees.

After complex and protracted litigation, the Massachusetts Supreme Court ruled in November 1917 that under terms of the McKay will, Harvard's liaison with M.I.T. was illicit. Students in the program at the time were permitted to complete the year's work before the arrangement was abandoned.

World War I violently interrupted what might have been a period of orderly growth. As soon as the United States broke off diplomatic relations with Germany in February 1917, President Maclaurin telegraphed the War Department offering the services of the Institute. Schools for Army and Navy aviators, for aviation engineers, for radio engineers, and for other specialized personnel were formed and the campus assumed the character of a military camp. There was extensive war-related research, though on a much smaller scale than in World War II. Professor Edward F. Miller built a steam-powered, 45-ton tank as a prototype of a new class of supermonsters (which never reached the battlefield). Nearly 5,000 students and alumni served in the military forces, about half of them as officers, and at least 2,300 served the government as civilians.

Hollis Godfrey '98 had a key role in the passage in 1916 of the National Defense Act, which established the Reserve Officers Training Corps. George E. Hale '90 was primarily responsible in that same year for formation of the National Research Council by the National Academy of Sciences and until after the war was chairman of the council. And President Maclaurin became educational director of the Student Army Training Corps, formed to prepare college men for officer training. (As it turned out, the draft age was lowered and the SATC really could do little more than provide barracks. Maclaurin had to fight for exemptions for medical students and technical specialists.)

13

A Culmination

77 "A cold, blustering Sunday morning of midwinter," wrote Professor William T. Sedgwick. "Fine, dry snow blowing past the housetops and filling the chilled air with whirling veils of frozen mist. Across the blanched and motionless Charles the great Technology buildings stood solemn, cold and gray in the eastern light." At 11:30 A.M., the eight oldest employees of the Institute bore the body of Richard C. Maclaurin from the President's House to the lobby of what is now known as the Maclaurin Building, to lie in state in academic gown under a pall of smilax and violets.

When the war was over, M.I.T. was facing a financial crisis and a campaign for $4,000,000 had to be launched. George Eastman agreed to give securities which would yield $200,000 a year if others would contribute $3,000,000. The goal was dramatically reached in 1920, the day before a dinner scheduled as a celebration — a special occasion on which the identity of Eastman, thus far known as "Mr. Smith," would be announced.

President Maclaurin wrote the speech he was to give but he could not attend the dinner. A cold he had contracted suddenly developed into a serious case of pneumonia. Professor William T. Sedgwick read the speech and Coleman du Pont disclosed the name of George Eastman — to the total surprise of alumni.

Having long strained his physical resources. President Maclaurin could not resist the illness. He died a few days later, on January 15, 1920, at the age of forty-nine. In doctor's hood and gown, he lay in state in the lobby of the building he had built as faculty, alumni, and students filed past to pay their respects.

78   The sun had come out at 1:30 P.M. when eight prominent seniors carried the casket to a hearse, to be taken to Old South Church for the funeral and then to Mount Auburn Cemetery. The pallbearers were Norris G. Abbott, Warren L. Cofren, John C. Nash, Edwin D. Ryer, Percy Bugbee, Count B. Capps, Scott H. Wells, and Kenneth F. Akers. Professor Robert Emmons Rogers wrote:

Bear him forth!
High on his young men's shoulders,
High between the long steady lines of his
    young men,
Slowly, steadily,
Out from the doors of the building he raised
    for us,
Into the blue and gold of the winter air,
Into the great wind sweeping the snow.

77

78

When the parent Institute moved to Cambridge, the Department of Architecture reveled in the inheritance of the old Rogers Building, which provided abundant space for exhibitions and other activities and became a center for Boston architects.

The department had started in that building, of course, but subsequently moved three times. In its first move, it gained by the innovation of electric lights, courtesy of Thomas A. Edison, who in 1887 gave a dynamo and 150 lamps to M.I.T. to use in teaching electrical engineering.

The course in architecture, without precedent in American colleges, was offered at the opening of the Institute but the Department of Architecture, the first in the country, was not formally organized until 1868. Meanwhile the professor, William Robert Ware, had gone to Europe and collected 2,000 photographs, 400 plaster casts, and 500 prints for use in classes. Eclecticism would reign for decades.

Louis H. Sullivan, the most innovative American architect of the nineteenth century, who studied at M.I.T. for one year, 1872–1873, found the department "a pale reflection of the École des Beaux-Arts," and fled from "fairy tales of long ago." But he learned "not only to draw, but to draw well." Drawing was a very important part of the curriculum. Eugene Létang, who came from the Beaux-Arts in 1871, was a passionate teacher of draftsmanship and an admirer of classical architecture.

Through a number of changes in the faculty, the Beaux-Arts tradition continued to dominate the department, though William Emerson, who was the head for twenty years, beginning in 1919, was receptive to new ideas. John E. Burchard '23 and Albert Bush-Brown, who was a professor of architectural history at M.I.T. before he became president of the Rhode Island School of Design, wrote in *The Architecture of America:*

The unreality of the late Beaux-Arts was not incompatible with American ambitions so long as wealthy clients wanted Old World magnificence. The crazy prosperity of the postwar Harding, Coolidge and Hoover era gave the Beaux-Arts student his last ready clientele. He could ignore social reform, slum problems, traffic problems. . . .

Nevertheless, there were forces of modernism at M.I.T. Two leaders of change were Lawrence B. Anderson '30 and Herbert L. Beckwith '26, members of the faculty whose Alumni Swimming Pool of 1938 was ahead of its time in collegiate architecture. Alvar Aalto came from Finland in 1940 as a research professor and later returned to design Baker House, one of his greatest buildings. M.I.T. was producing architects who would be among the nation's most eminent — Edward Durrell Stone '27, Harry M. Weese '38, I. M. Pei '40, Gordon Bunshaft '33, of Skidmore, Owings & Merrill in New York, and Walter A. Netsch Jr. '43 and William E. Hartmann '37 of the Skidmore office in Chicago.

14

Architects and Planners

The Department of Architecture became the School of Architecture in 1932 and a division of city planning was formed, the second such program in the country. Harvard's was the first, having started in 1925. The new Rogers Building, with its great portico providing an entrance on Massachusetts Avenue, was completed in 1938 and the school moved into it that fall, enabling students to take courses in other departments without the inconvenience of traveling from Copley Square.

79   As seen through the eyes of Samuel V. Chamberlain '18, who studied architecture there, the old Rogers Building had a gracious air in its old age. Chamberlain, a superb etcher and photographer and an authority on French cooking, published more than eighty books.

80

81

80   The first thesis done by an M.I.T. architecture student was the design of a waterworks, with gushing fountains and a standpipe in monumental form topped with a lightning rod. The student was Henry A. Phillips '73.

81   The architectural drawing room on the fourth floor of the Rogers Building in 1874. President Rogers had had some arguments with the architects, Jonathan and William G. Preston, about changes in the roof in order to get that fourth floor. He noted: "These architects are great plagues when they persist in disregarding utility for the sake of their notions of outside appearance."

The school did not fully enter its modern period until 1944, when William Wilson Wurster '17 became dean. Its name was changed to School of Architecture and Planning and, in addition to the Department of Architecture, a new Department of City and Regional Planning was formed. Through the administrations of three other deans, Pietro Belluschi, Lawrence Anderson, and William L. Porter, who received the Ph.D. in planning from M.I.T. in 1969, the program was greatly broadened.

With Harvard, the Joint Center for Urban Studies for advanced research was established in 1959. Increasing attention was given to visual design. The Center for Advanced Visual Studies was organized in 1967, with Gyorgy Kepes as the first director. Programs in photography and film-making were inaugurated. Studies in the history, theory, and criticism of art and architecture were steadily strengthened. Courses were designed to attract students from all parts of M.I.T., not just those who would be professional architects and planners.

82   When Constant Désiré Despradelle arrived from France to join the faculty in 1893, he visited the Chicago World's Fair and was so inspired that he designed this "Beacon of Progress" — "to glorify the American Nation." It won the first gold medal at the Paris Salon in 1900. If built, it would have been 1,500 feet high, half again higher than the Eiffel Tower and higher than anything that exists today.

83   In the twenties and thirties, Johan Selmer-Larsen taught the modeling of ornamentation for buildings.

82

83

But the greatest change came through the new attention to social consequences, environmental problems, the needs of minorities. Dean Anderson
observed in 1968: "Students of planning see the old policies of public
housing, zoning, and urban renewal as ineffectual, if not sometimes harmful
controls on urbanization; students of architecture see the stylish work of
prominent architects as ephemeral and irrelevant to the wider problems of
environmental improvement."

The name of the Department of City and Regional Planning was changed
to Department of Urban Studies and Planning, expressing a new orientation.
A Laboratory of Architecture and Planning was established in 1973 as the
research center for the school, with Dean Porter as director. The volume of
research, which had been relatively small, has increased to more than
$2,000,000 a year. Research is directed not only at traditional problems of
housing but at such new, important areas as architectural design for the
elderly and public service systems. Throughout, computer techniques are
extensively applied. The school has a concern for a "more human" environment for the everyday life of all citizens.

84   The modern look in architecture had
arrived when Ieoh M. Pei '40 executed this
thesis — a Chinese community center, with
bamboo to be used in its construction. Pei
went on to the design of some of the world's
most notable buildings, including three at
M.I.T.

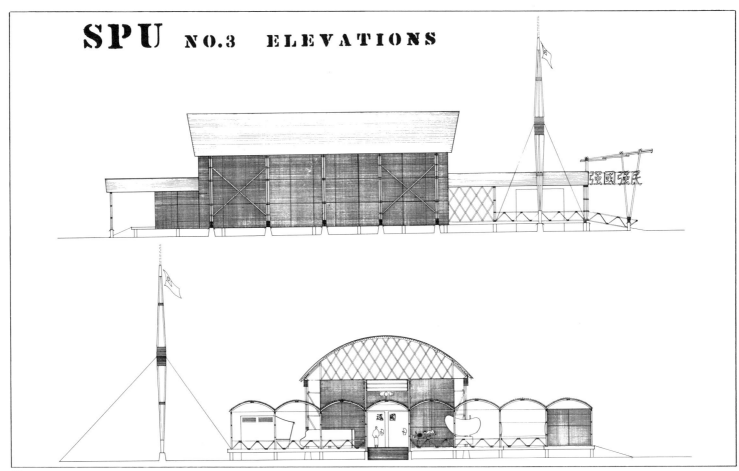

85   In developing a plan for Rockport, Massachusetts, Elizabeth Ellis (left) and Jennifer Shakespeare helped build a detailed relief plan of the town. Lawrence Susskind, associate professor of urban studies and planning, led fourteen students in working with the community to analyze the town's problems.

86   Tunney Lee (rear center), associate professor of urban design, guided architecture and planning students in a study in 1975 of the Dudley Street station area in Boston, which was on the verge of extensive change through the removal of elevated tracks and the relocation of the station. Here the group lunches with three high school students (in the foreground) from the black community to get their ideas on how the neighborhood should be developed for the good of all.

85

86

In the age of the conquest of space, the conquest of the air may seem to have been prosaic, but it also required bold ideas, patient research, and innovative men. M.I.T. contributed all three.

Research started in 1896, when a student built a small wind tunnel using the air current from the Institute's ventilating system. The wind speed produced was only 15 miles an hour but several students were able to do theses in studies of effects on various surfaces. The tunnel may have been the first in the United States. Within a few years students began building gliders. They organized the M.I.T. Aero Club in 1909 and won a cup in a glider meet the next year. Some of their flights were conducted on the Charles River when it was frozen over. The operator wore skates.

Consequential research began, however, with Jerome C. Hunsaker, who became one of the great men of aeronautics. He graduated from Annapolis in 1908, the same year that Orville Wright gave a convincing demonstration to the Army by flying an airplane for one hour and two minutes. Hunsaker was sent by the Navy to M.I.T. for graduate study in ship construction, but by the time he received the master's degree in 1912 he had become enamored of ships that fly in the air.

15

Aeronautics and Airmen

87   Jerome Hunsaker's first wind tunnel at M.I.T. was 4′ by 4′ in cross section and had a chain-driven black walnut propeller that produced a wind speed of 40 miles an hour. It was the first research facility on the Cambridge campus, being installed in a shed before the main building was completed.

87

88

89

Interest in aeronautics was growing at M.I.T. — in part because of Hunsaker's enthusiasm — and in 1913 President Maclaurin asked the Navy to assign him to the development of courses. Hunsaker was sent to Europe to learn of research and education there.

In France, Hunsaker met Alexandre Gustave Eiffel (he had translated Eiffel's classic treatise on aerodynamics the year before and had found some errors in the calculations) and studied wind tunnel experiments in the Eiffel laboratory. In Germany, he met the young Dutchman Anthony Fokker, who was building a monoplane, and he took a cruise in the Zeppelin. In England he became acquainted with such aviation leaders as Handley Page and he worked for a time with the wind tunnel group in the National Physical Laboratory at Teddington.

Returning to M.I.T. in 1914, Hunsaker proceeded to build a wind tunnel similar to the one at Teddington, probably the first really effective wind tunnel in America. His assistant in the project was handsome young Donald W. Douglas '14, who had just graduated in mechanical engineering. He also had attended Annapolis but was more interested in airplanes than ships and transferred to M.I.T. After working with Hunsaker for a year he went into industry and became one of the giants among aircraft builders.

Meanwhile, Hunsaker had inaugurated the aeronautical engineering courses, the first of their kind in the country, and on the basis of his wind tunnel work won his own doctoral degree, the first in aeronautics awarded by M.I.T. The Navy called him to Washington in 1917 to direct the new Aircraft Division in the Construction Department. In fact, he was in charge

88   Jerome C. Hunsaker '12 pioneered in aeronautical engineering and for more than a decade was head of the Department of Mechanical Engineering.

89   During World War I, M.I.T. conducted special ground schools for Army and Navy aviators and engineers.

of all Navy aircraft construction during World War I and was responsible for many innovations. He designed the NC-4, which flew to Lisbon and England, the first airplane to cross the Atlantic.

Hunsaker's tunnel was leased to the Army during the war and M.I.T. conducted special schools for both Army and Navy aviators and engineers. Leroy R. Grumman and Juan T. Trippe, whose names would become famous in aviation, were among those sent by the Navy to the Institute. Edwin E. Aldrin Sr. '17 received a master's degree in aeronautics and was assigned by the Army as an instructor. He later received a doctorate and had a useful career but would be best known as the father of Edwin ''Buzz'' Aldrin Jr. '63 (who also was granted a doctorate at M.I.T.), one of the first two men to land on the moon.

Another World War I student and instructor, Edward P. Warner '17, went to Langley Field to initiate construction of the first NACA wind tunnel. He returned to M.I.T. in 1920 to take charge of aeronautical engineering, which was now under the administration of the Physics Department. After six years he left to become assistant secretary of the Navy and, later, editor of *Aviation.*

Some of the most brilliant students remained as members of the faculty — Shatswell Ober '16, Otto C. Koppen '24, and John R. Markham '18. And one of the greatest — Charles Stark Draper '26 — who would devise a way to navigate to the moon.

The Navy and Jerry Hunsaker became deeply interested during the twenties in lighter-than-air craft. Hunsaker designed the Shenandoah, the first American Zeppelin-type ship, which crashed during a storm two years after it was built. That disaster convinced him that better understanding of the weather was needed — and better means of communications with aircraft. To help on the latter, he joined Bell Telephone Laboratories and conceived the communications network that was adopted for airways. Then he went to the Goodyear-Zeppelin Corporation to build the Akron and Macon, both of which were doomed and ended the Navy's enthusiasm for lighter-than-air craft.

In his deep concern about weather problems, Hunsaker urged M.I.T. to develop studies in meteorology. Courses in meteorology had once been given to graduate students in aeronautical engineering but had been dropped. They were resumed in 1928 and M.I.T. enlisted a promising young Swede, Carl-Gustaf A. Rossby (who came to be recognized as the father of modern meteorological science), to establish a program similar to the one at the Geophysics Institute at Bergen, Norway, of which he was a product.

Up till that time, weather soundings had been taken by means of kites and free-floating balloons, not always a reliable method. M.I.T. started sending an airplane up to 17,000 feet — very high for that time — to obtain data. The pilots were Draper and Daniel C. Sayre '23, a professor of aeronautical engineering.

90   James H. Doolittle, who received the Sc.D. degree in 1925, accomplished the first blind flying and landing. This picture was made in 1930 just after he set a new transcontinental speed record of 11 hours and 15 minutes. He led the amazing surprise ''Shangri-La'' bombing raid on Tokyo from the carrier *Hornet,* had several commands, and became a lieutenant general. He was an active member of the M.I.T. Corporation for a dozen years.

90

91   Carl-Gustaf A. Rossby (left), the father of modern meteorology, joined the aeronautical engineering faculty in 1928 and daily flights were inaugurated to get weather data as high as 17,000 feet. In the center is Karl O. Lange, director of the flights, holding a meteorograph carried under the wing to record temperature, relative humidity, and barometric pressure. Professor Daniel C. Sayre (right) and Charles S. Draper were pilots.

92   Karl Lange and Daniel Sayre with the Warner-Cessna used for weather flights. Until then, meteorologists had depended on kites and balloons for gathering data above the ground.

91

92

In 1933, Hunsaker returned to M.I.T. as head of the Department of Mechanical Engineering, of which aeronautical engineering had become a part, and of the Department of Aeronautical Engineering when it was established in 1939. He continued to have an influential role in determining national aviation policies and in 1941 he became chairman of the National Advisory Committee for Aeronautics, succeeding Vannevar Bush when he became chief of all wartime research. After his retirement from the faculty in 1952 Hunsaker kept an office in the Guggenheim building. Still debonair in his eighties, he remained in touch with leaders of aeronautics and regularly went to the Institute.

16

Powerful Catalysts

Although the Chemistry Department began offering a course in chemical engineering in 1888, the Department of Chemical Engineering (the first in any college) was not established until 1920.

Meanwhile, however, M.I.T. had become strong in the field. The Research Laboratory of Applied Chemistry was formed by William H. Walker in 1906. Ten years later, the School of Chemical Engineering Practice (to train students at industrial plants) was organized at the instigation of Arthur D. Little '85, founder of the first industrial consulting firm.

The new department was headed by Warren K. Lewis '05, of legendary fame as a teacher. Walker, Lewis, and William H. McAdams '17 wrote the first comprehensive textbook, *Principles of Chemical Engineering,* and M.I.T. students used it in mimeographed form before it was published.

One of the students was Eric Hodgins '22, who turned to writing and became publisher of *Fortune.* "Doc" Lewis let him graduate (so the story goes) on condition that he never attempt to practice chemical engineering. His recollections in *Trolley to the Moon* of the time of Walker, Lewis, and McAdams are graphic:

It isn't too much to say that these three men, particularly the first two, aided by the distinguished chemist-alumnus Arthur Dehon Little, invented chemical engineering and brought forth, out of such empirical and messy nineteenth-century arts as leather tanning, glue boiling and papermaking, an engineering discipline susceptible to mathematical and other scientific manipulation. Dr. Little had been visited by inspiration a few years earlier and had proposed the concept of "unit operations" — heat transfer, filtration, distillation, etc. — which not only brought order out of chaos to the chemical industry but made the engineering of chemistry a logical entity. And Doc Lewis was a teacher of teachers.

93

93   William H. Walker was one of the founders of chemical engineering and the first director of the Division of Industrial Co-operation and Research.

94   Arthur D. Little pioneered in industrial research and was influential in developing chemical engineering at M.I.T., especially the School of Chemical Engineering Practice. He served as president of the Alumni Association and was a member of the Corporation from 1912 until his death in 1935. In his will he left controlling interest in Arthur D. Little, Inc., in trust to M.I.T., for the benefit of the Institute and to ensure the research firm's continued independence. In 1953 the controlling stock in the company, 5,543 shares, was sold to an employees' trust for $1,330,320.

95   Warren K. Lewis "always looked as if he were going to explode." This picture was made after his retirement in 1948. He died in 1975 at the age of ninety-two.

94

95

He wore the same necktie three months at a time, and his glittering gold-framed spectacles sat only slightly askew on a somewhat lumpy nose. His face usually bore the slightest suggestion, only slight, of a frown. When he entered a classroom he neither strolled nor stalked; he just walked in. Nevertheless, when he did, an instantaneous hush fell, for there was not one undergraduate who was not terrified of Doc. I have spent some years trying to account for this, and the best I can come up with was that Doc always looked as if he were going to explode, and a shard from him was going to rip through your intestines any minute. Yet I knew him, so it was to turn out, not only as an undergraduate but for twenty-five years thereafter — and he never did explode.

In scrabbling for funds after World War I, M.I.T. formed a Division of Industrial Cooperation and Research, with Dr. Walker as the director. Under what was known as the "Technology Plan," the division entered into contracts with industry by which the faculty assisted in solving research problems. There was grumbling among some professors that the Institute was being prostituted and that attention to practical problems would interfere with pure research, but the scheme formalized a policy of continuing benefit. DIC evolved into the Industrial Liaison Program and the Office of Sponsored Programs, which encouraged interaction with industry and growth in many M.I.T. activities.

In his research and as a private consultant, Lewis made enormous contributions to the chemical industry, especially in the development of new methods for refining petroleum, such as continuous rectification and cata-

96   Raymond F. Baddour '49, now head of the department and Lammot du Pont Professor, developed advanced separation methods for industrial use.

97   A new building, designed by I. M. Pei & Partners, was completed for the Department of Chemical Engineering in 1975.

96

97

lytic cracking. Just before World War II, he and Edwin R. Gilliland '33 invented the fluid-bed method of catalytic cracking, which boosted production of aviation gasoline and is used to produce most American gasoline today.

The Department of Chemical Engineering has graduated many industrial leaders and its faculty members have made significant research contributions. Walter G. Whitman '17 conceived the two-film theory of mass transport between phases, widely used in industry and in air pollution control. Hoyt C. Hottel '24 developed scientific methods of industrial furnace design and founded the Fuels Research Laboratory, which pioneered in flame kinetics and heat transfer. Thomas K. Sherwood '24, who served as dean of engineering, wrote the first authoritative texts on mass transfer and applied mathematics in chemical engineering. Raymond F. Baddour '49 developed advanced separation methods. Whitman and Gilliland each served as head of the department and Baddour is head now.

In recent years, chemical engineering has given special attention to environmental problems, such as soot, carbon monoxide, nitric acid, and wastes, and to medical-related areas such as enzyme technology. Edward W. Merrill '47 has been especially active in the latter areas, and developed a Viscometer for measuring properties of the blood and an aerosol generator for treatment of hyaline membrane disease.

In 1970 the department celebrated its fiftieth anniversary with a great convocation chaired by Ralph Landau '41. One notable result was the decision to raise, under a national committee headed by J. Kenneth Jamieson '31, private funds for a commodious new departmental building. In 1975, this building was the newest on campus.

The death of President Maclaurin in 1920 had been a shock to all those who loved him and a severe blow to M.I.T., which would miss his leadership even more than could then be realized. The nation was entering a postwar transitional period, one of sudden acceleration and rapid change. The Institute needed a strong president.

Elihu Thomson was enlisted as acting president. A member of the Corporation for more than a score of years and honored with the title of nonresident professor, he was an inventor comparable to Thomas Edison in accomplishment if not in fame. The Thomson-Houston Electric Company in Lynn, founded primarily on his inventions (he had some five hundred), had been merged with the Edison Company to form the General Electric Company. At the age of sixty-six, he was chief consulting engineer for General Electric and living in semiretirement at Swampscott. He agreed to sign diplomas and other papers that M.I.T. might send him.

A year passed before the Institute found a new president: Dr. Ernest F. Nichols, a physicist who had been president of Dartmouth College for seven years and was currently director of physical science at the Nela Park Research Laboratories of the National Lamp Works in Cleveland. By coincidence, it was he who, while on the faculty of Columbia University, had been responsible for bringing Maclaurin to the United States.

17

The Transitional Twenties

98

98   Elihu Thomson, twice acting president of M.I.T., was particularly interested in using the 10-inch telescope he had built and installed at his home in Swampscott.

Dr. Nichols was inaugurated in 1921 and almost immediately laid low by heart disease. After five months, he resigned. (He died in 1924 while giving a paper before the National Academy of Sciences.) Elihu Thomson again became acting president.

After another year, the Corporation selected sixty-one-year-old Samuel W. Stratton, who had been director of the U.S. Bureau of Standards since 1901. In fact, he organized the bureau, having been recruited from the University of Chicago by Henry S. Pritchett (superintendent of the Coast and Geodetic Survey before he became president of M.I.T.) to make a study of how the Division of Weights and Measures could be modernized to meet the changing industrial and scientific needs of the country. (Stratton was succeeded at the Bureau of Standards by George K. Burgess '96, who had taught physics.)

Stratton, who took office in 1923, was not an innovator. A bachelor, he installed a machine shop in the basement of the President's House and he liked nothing better than tinkering there. Yet there were pockets of lively activity at the Institute, one of them being the English Department. Eric Hodgins was especially enthusiastic about Frank Aydelotte, who later became president of Swarthmore College and then director of the Princeton Institute for Advanced Study. Hodgins wrote: "It was he who devised the mandatory English and history course for second-year students, and a

99   For the first time, seniors wore caps and gowns and received diplomas from the hand of the president in 1923. Theodore M. Edison has just been given his. In the audience was his father, Thomas Edison, who, true to legend, snoozed.

100   The alumni reunion boat trip to Georges Island in 1925 was enlivened by a mad professor, Xerxes Y. Zizziter, who claimed to have an "apparatus for the disintegration of the atom and the release of its energy."

100

101

102

beauty it was both for what it offered the student and because it was also a gun-spiker for the enemies of Culture hidden here and there in the more hard-bitten core of the faculty."

Hodgins was even more enthusiastic about caustic, iconoclastic Robert Emmons "Tubby" Rogers. He wrote: "After a while it dawned on me that I had had the incredible luck of falling under the influence of a genial anarchist. Of all the shapers of my early life, he was the major one."

With his zest for literature and good living, Tubby was the yeast that leavened the lives of a great many Tech boys between 1913 and 1941. One of them was Julius A. Stratton (not related to Samuel Stratton), who graduated in 1923 with such a strong bent toward humanities that he went to the University of Toulouse and started work on a doctoral thesis on the influence of science in nineteenth-century French literature. He later became a physicist but not at a loss of taste for belles lettres.

Tubby Rogers, in addition to teaching, was editor of *Technology Review* until 1922. Graduating that year, Hodgins became managing editor, with Harold E. Lobdell '17, assistant dean of students, as editor. Another disciple of Tubby Rogers, James Rhyne Killian Jr., editor of *The Tech,* joined the staff of *Technology Review* after graduating in 1926. When Hodgins left, Killian succeeded him as managing editor and later became editor, preparing (though he couldn't have known it then) to be one of the Institute's greatest presidents.

Tubby is most widely remembered for his advice to the graduates of 1929, which spiced the front pages of newspapers throughout the country — a recipe for success: "Be a snob, and marry the boss's daughter."

The advice was offered at the senior banquet, doubtless with facetiousness appropriate to the occasion, and Rogers didn't know that a newspaper reporter was present. It provoked public indignation, but Tubby defended

103

104

104   David A. Shepard was president of the Class of 1926 and James R. Killian Jr., editor of *The Tech,* was a leading member of the class. Shepard joined Standard Oil of New Jersey, became executive vice-president, and has been a member of the M.I.T. Corporation since 1951. Killian remained, as editor, president, chairman.

himself in *Technology Review:* "I stand by my guns. I want Technology men to remember that each one of them is the sole survivor of one hundred boys who started in the public school system with them and have dropped off. They should, obviously, represent an intellectual aristocracy."

Such sentiments might have gotten Tubby Rogers hanged — in effigy, at least — during the egalitarian hysteria of forty years later, when the vulgarity of the much-admired "street people" became the model for revolutionary patter on the campus. But in the twenties — certainly in the months before the 1929 stock market crash — the ideal of most college people was to be collegiate ("nothing intermejiate," proclaimed a popular ditty), sophisticated, with a speakeasy vocabulary, and the common ambition was to be successful in business.

Among M.I.T. people, no one was more successful than two members of the Class of 1895, Alfred P. Sloan Jr., who was president of General Motors, and Gerard Swope, president of General Electric. The peak of Sloan's success at General Motors and of his enormous contributions to M.I.T. would come later. Swope's influence was felt very soon.

In an article about Swope, Willis Whitney pointed out that the modern industrial corporation was "a smoothly running machine" and that Swope

105

105   Smith D. Turner '26, a chemical engineer who joined Standard Oil, offers photographic evidence of odd chemical experiments
in Atkinson, Senior House, in 1927. He iden-
tifies the experimenters as Bill Phillips, Freddie
Bodden, Gus Lobo, Sparky Turner, Jerry Eaton,
Hersch Hyde, and Pete Guscio.

was the kind of man who could run such a machine. Swope became a member of the Executive Committee of the M.I.T. Corporation and saw that the
Institute was not running smoothly with Sam Stratton as president. It was, in
fact, running down. Swope and a selection committee proceeded with a
search for a new chief executive.

Two physicists were regarded with special favor: Arthur H. Compton of
the University of Chicago, who had won the Nobel Prize three years before,
and his older brother, Karl Taylor Compton, head of the physics department
at Princeton University. It happened that Karl was well known at General
Electric. Back in 1916, when he was a young assistant professor at Princeton,
Willis Whitney, looking for brainpower, asked him to become a consultant
to the Research Laboratory, so once a month Compton visited Schenectady.
He worked on papers on electrical discharges with GE's Irving Langmuir, one
of the most respected physicists in the country.

Swope asked Compton for his opinion of the General Electric laboratory
and Karl responded with a detailed letter. Then, to Compton's surprise,
Swope asked if he would be interested in becoming president of M.I.T.
Compton felt he was not qualified as an administrator or public speaker and
he was enthusiastic about his career ahead at Princeton. However, he discussed the offer with his friend, Frank B. Jewett '03, president of Bell
Telephone Laboratories and a member of the M.I.T. Corporation, and
decided to accept.

On March 12, 1930, Stratton was elected to the newly created office of
chairman of the Corporation and Karl Compton was elected president. The
action changed the Institute's future.

18

Electrical Dynamists

In 1882, the year that M.I.T. inaugurated the first course in electrical engineering, New England's first electric street lights were turned on in Lynn, powered by a dynamo built by Elihu Thomson.

By the nineties, the power industry was booming and there was a stampede of students into electrical engineering, still offered as a physics course. In 1902 the Department of Electrical Engineering was organized and installed in a new building, the Augustus Lowell Laboratory. In 1921, its enrollment became the largest of any M.I.T. department (and has been ever since).

In command of the department from 1907 to 1935 was Dugald C. Jackson, a professor of legendary toughness. He met his match in Vannevar Bush, who later wrote: "I owed him much, and I was exceedingly grateful to him, though we battled often and vigorously. He was at times a fire-eater. . . ."

Van Bush was the grandson of Cape Cod sea captains and the son of a Universalist clergyman. He had energy and brains. While an undergraduate at Tufts College he took out his first patent — for a surveying device mounted on bicycle wheels — and after graduating was an instructor in mathematics.

Having saved enough money for one year of graduate study, Bush undertook to qualify for a doctorate in electrical engineering at M.I.T. in that one year so that he could get a better job and could afford to be married. Professor Jackson was extremely skeptical but accepted him as a graduate student. At the end of the year, in 1916, Bush had indeed earned a doctorate. During World War I, Bush did research for the Navy, developing a magnetic device for detecting submarines. Because of faulty administrative coordination, the device was never used effectively — providing a lesson that he would remember when he became chief of all U.S. research during World War II.

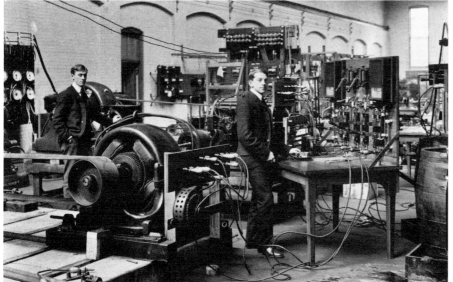

106

106   The Augustus Lowell Laboratory for Electrical Engineering, which opened in 1902, was a memorial to a Corporation member, from 1873 until his death in 1900, given by his five children: Amy Lowell, the poet; Percival Lowell, the astronomer; Abbott Lawrence Lowell, who taught history at Tech for a year, was a Corporation member from 1896 to 1943, and who was president of Harvard; and Mrs. William Putnam and Mrs. T. J. Bowlker. It generated electricity to light various buildings as well as providing "current of any required amount" for experiments.

107

107   Dugald Jackson, "at times a fire-eater," was head of the Department of Electrical Engineering from 1907 to 1935.

108   As a boy in Chelsea, Massachusetts, Vannevar Bush had his own workshop, with shelves in a Quaker Oats box for chemicals and odd treasures in salt-cod boxes. On the bench is what appears to be a dry cell hooked up to a clock. He tinkered and learned.

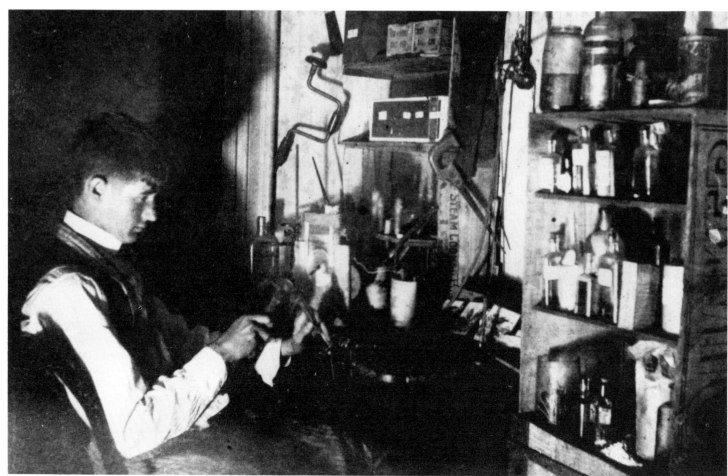

108

In 1919, at the age of twenty-nine, Bush joined the M.I.T. faculty as associate professor of power transmission. He also became involved with a small company in Medford, American Research and Development Corporation, which was pioneering in the manufacture of radio components. Through a series of corporate permutations, into which Bush introduced his old Tufts roommate, Laurence K. Marshall, as entrepreneur, the venture led to the formation of Raytheon Company.

One of Bush's graduate students, Edward L. Bowles '22, was headed for the power industry. In his laboratory work he needed a vacuum tube of a special kind and Bush arranged for him to build it at the AMRAD plant. Bowles wound up making several tubes and deciding to be a radio engineer.

The Department of Electrical Engineering at that time was strongly oriented toward power generation and transmission. Radio was regarded as a novelty of transient interest. Bowles, now an instructor, recognized it as an important emerging field and, with Carlton E. Tucker '18, developed a new curriculum in communications.

109   Vannevar Bush (left) needed four operators to run the Product Integraph in 1927. They were Walter F. Kershaw, Frank G. Kear '27, Harold L. Hazen '24, and Murray F. Gardner '24.

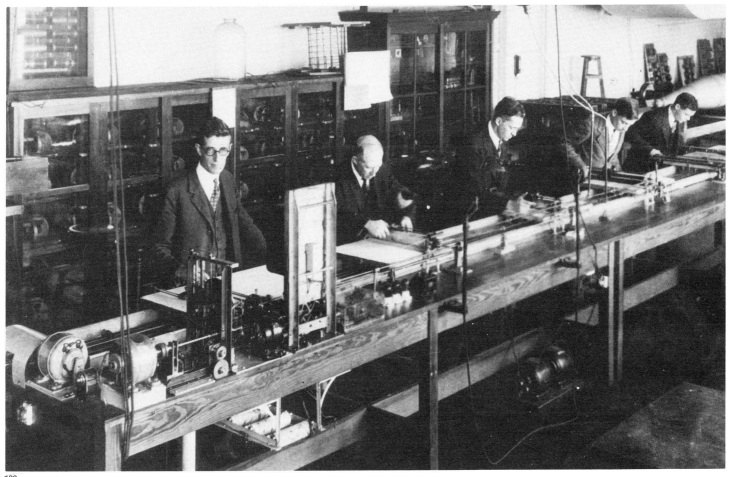

As a senior in 1923 (and secretary of the Radio Society, which operated a transmitter powerful enough to be heard in Hawaii), Julius A. Stratton did his thesis under Bowles, collaborating with James K. Clapp '23. Stratton had built his own wireless set as a boy in Seattle and then went to sea as an operator. He became a research associate in communications but wanted to explore the vast territory of electromagnetism and would later go to Zurich for a doctorate in physics.

Bowles, Stratton, and Clapp were among those who became involved in one of M.I.T.'s most interesting enterprises — research at Round Hill on Buzzards Bay. Round Hill had belonged to Hetty Green, notorious as the world's richest and most miserly woman. After she died, her son, Colonel Edward Howland Robinson Green, built a huge mansion on the estate and devoted his inherited wealth to the things that interested him most, such as radio, aeronautics, whaling ships, and pretty girls, though not always in that order. He built his own radio station, WMAF, and in 1923 inaugurated the first American network broadcasts, with programs transmitted from New York by telephone line and then beamed from Round Hill to New England.

In 1925, Colonel Green invited M.I.T. to use Round Hill for research. Although radio was becoming commonplace, much was yet to be learned about its characteristics and possibilities, especially in short wavelengths. M.I.T. established an experimental station, 1XV, with Bowles in charge. Needing a fixed position in the air for testing antennas, Bowles arranged with Paul W. Litchfield '96, president of the Goodyear-Zeppelin Corporation, for the loan of a dirigible, the *Mayflower,* for two summers. Experimental apparatus was sent aloft in the dirigible.

Air operations introduced the problem of fog, which Round Hill had in abundance, and this led into new areas of research. Stratton and Henry G. Houghton '27 conducted studies of the transmission of radio and light through fog. Houghton's studies of fog resulted in a method of dissipating it by spraying salts in the moisture-laden air. (Bowles recalls with amusement that spraying nozzles were patterned after the spraying apparatus of the skunk — with which he had become familiar as a boy trapper in the Ozarks.) Houghton's interest in the weather grew until he chose to become a meteorologist.

The spraying method of fog dissipation worked, but methods of navigating in the fog held more promise, and Bowles pioneered in research on the use of microwaves for this purpose. Julius Stratton, whose interest was focused on electromagnetic theory, transferred to the physics faculty in 1930. He and Bowles supervised research by Wilmer L. Barrow '29, who demonstrated that ultra-high-frequency waves could be transmitted through pipes and who developed an electromagnetic horn to send out a beam. Bowles, Barrow, and others devised a microwave landing system, which was to have been installed experimentally at the Boston airport. World War II turned priorities to other matters in which the microwave research paid off enormously.

110   Because his mother was too stingy to call a doctor, Colonel E. H. R. Green had to have an infected leg amputated. After Hetty Green's death, he had a specially built electric car, which he called the Cream Puff, to ride about his estate at Round Hill.

110

111   The array of nozzles for spraying salts to dissipate fog at Round Hill. In the background is the famous whaler *Charles W. Morgan,* which had been in Colonel Green's great-grandfather's fleet sailing from New Bedford.

111

Meanwhile, Vannevar Bush had been adventuring in the realm of mathematical machines. The incentive was that the increasing complexity of electric power transmission systems demanded mathematics of staggering difficulty. Under the direction of Bush, Herbert R. Stewart '24 and Frank D. Gage '22 built a breadboard model of an analog computer that was known as the Product Integraph. Rather than counting numbers, as digital computers do today, it solved problems by measuring varying electrical voltages and mechanical movement. Harold L. Hazen '24 showed how the machine could be improved to deal with more complex equations and a second model was built. A writer at the time described it as "virtually a man-made mind" which "transcends human reasoning in its ability to write the answer to mathematical problems too complex for the human brain to solve."

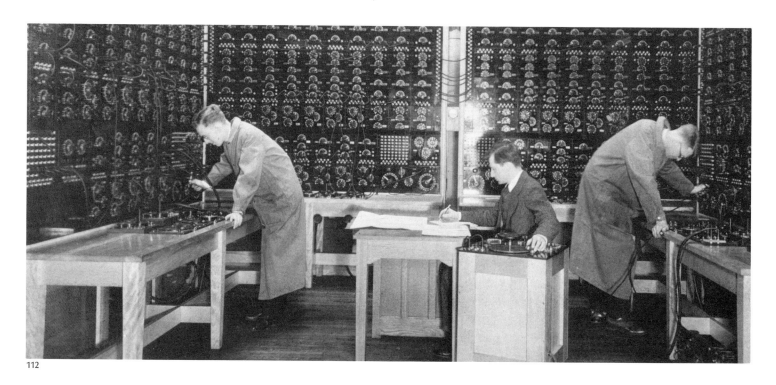

112

A more complicated and efficient machine, called the Differential Analyzer, was then built and became the prototype for machines built elsewhere. A second version, the Rockefeller Differential Analyzer, built in the thirties, was a monster weighing 100 tons, with 2,000 electronic tubes, 200 miles of wire, and 150 motors. During World War II it was operated twenty-four hours a day on radar, fire control, and other problems.

Various efforts at dealing with complex computation were made. Norbert Wiener, genius in the Department of Mathematics, was struck by an idea while at the theater one night and walked out on the play to concentrate on his thinking. The next day he told Bush about his concept of an optical computing device. Truman S. Gray '29 developed it as the Photo-Electric Integraph. Another graduate student, Gordon S. Brown '31, applied the notion to a machine he called the Cinema Integraph because it employed motion picture film.

Experience with such analog devices would have consequences, introducing Gordon Brown, for instance, to the field of automatic controls, in which he was a leading innovator. The development of digital computers would have to wait. Meanwhile there had been educational change. To some professors, electric power was paramount, but Bowles, Stratton, and others argued successfully for emphasis on teaching basic principles that could be applied to power, communications, or other electric systems. Electrical engineering professors worked with physicists in revising the curriculum to deal with emerging theory and practice. "Electronics" was taught for the first time.

112   Harold L. Hazen (center) supervised the construction of the Network Analyzer to simulate a power network. At left is Samuel H. Caldwell '25, and at right, Sidney E. Caldwell '32.

113

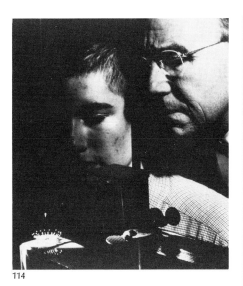

114

115

113　Gordon S. Brown '31, as head of the Department of Electrical Engineering and then dean of the School of Engineering, led in educational innovation and in the development of servomechanisms and computer technology.

114　Harold E. Edgerton never ceased to find joy in using the strobe to photograph such phenomena as splashing milk to interest freshman like Peter A. Konde '66. This composite picture was made by Gjon Mili '27.

115　Gjon Mili began his career as a lighting engineer but after experimenting with Edgerton strobes became one of the world's greatest photographers. From time to time he returned to M.I.T. to do some teaching.

Changes continued when Dugald Jackson's partner, Edward L. Moreland '07, became head of the department in 1935 and then became dean of engineering three years later, to be succeeded by Harold Hazen (later dean of the Graduate School).

Gordon Brown, Australian-born and incisively articulate, was appointed head of the department in 1952 and demonstrated the toughness of Dugald Jackson and Van Bush. The basement of Building 10 was cluttered with dynamos and motors, some of which, like the steam engines in mechanical engineering, dated to 1916. He got rid of them. Under his leadership, David C. White and others developed a "generalized machine," a unit not much larger than a vacuum cleaner that could be used in teaching the concepts of any kind of rotating machine. Westinghouse Electric Company cooperated in manufacturing it as a tool for a new approach in engineering schools throughout the country. Brown became dean of engineering in 1959, carrying the banner of reform to other departments.

Computers, semiconductors, and other new developments had an enormous impact on research and teaching in the department while Jerome B. Wiesner, Peter Elias '44, Louis D. Smullin '39, and Wilbur R. Davenport Jr. '43 each served as head. Expansion into new fields required increasing space, and this was provided in 1973 by the completion of the $17,500,000 Sherman Fairchild Building, named for the founder of the Fairchild camera company. The department got a new name in 1975. About a third of its students were studying computer science, and it was renamed the Department of Electrical Engineering and Computer Science.

116   The Sherman Fairchild Building for Electrical Engineering, completed in 1973, the largest building since the main buildings were finished in 1916.

Karl Taylor Compton had felt most at home in a laboratory, but he soon demonstrated as much talent for administration as for experimental physics. This was hardly surprising, considering his early nurture. His father, Elias Compton, was psychology professor and dean at the College of Wooster in Ohio. A small Presbyterian institution, the school was one of consecrated scholarship and the Comptons were deeply religious, not merely in form but in their devotion to each other, to students, and to altruistic, wholesome, and creative living.

The four Compton children all graduated from Wooster and the three brothers earned Ph.D.'s at Princeton. Wilson M. Compton, the second oldest, was an economist and became president of Washington State College. Arthur H. Compton, long a physicist at the University of Chicago, became chancellor of Washington University in St. Louis. Their sister, Mary, went to India as an educational missionary and married a Wooster schoolmate, Herbert Rice, later principal of Allahabad Christian College. And — of extreme importance — Karl Compton was married to Margaret Hutchinson, daughter of a Greek and biblical scholar at the University of Minnesota. She had been a campus YWCA director and shared with the Comptons a love of humanity and enthusiasm for constructive life.

When Gerard Swope was trying to persuade Compton to accept the M.I.T. presidency, Compton expressed doubt about going to an institution that provided so little support for physics research. Swope pointed out that as president he could make the physics budget as big as he liked. Upon his arrival at the Institute, Compton gave prompt attention to the department, which had lost its vitality and was primarily a service department for engineering students, although this was a period of excitement throughout the world in physics. The importance of the arrival of a man of Compton's prestige and accomplishment could not be exaggerated. He had been president of the American Physical Society from 1927 to 1929 and was a leader in the organization of the American Institute of Physics, of which he would become the first chairman in 1931. Eminent physicists of the day, invited to pick the six outstanding American scientists, chose Karl Compton along with Arthur Compton and A. A. Michelson of Chicago, Percy A. Bridgman of Harvard, Robert A. Millikan of Caltech and R. W. Wood of Johns Hopkins.

Well acquainted in the field, President Compton enlisted as new head of the Department of Physics twenty-nine-year-old John C. Slater, professor of theoretical physics at Harvard. To lead an initiative in experimental physics George R. Harrison, a friend of Slater during postdoctoral days at Harvard, was brought from Stanford University to be director of the Research Laboratory of Experimental Physics. Both provided the kind of spark that Compton wanted. Slater would be head of the department for more than two decades and three Nobel physicists would come from among the graduate students. Harrison was productive in research and would serve with distinction as dean of science during the crucial years from 1942 to 1963.

19

A Radiant Leader

117   In 1930, Edwin H. Blashfield '69 painted this allegory in Walker Memorial (he had done other murals six years earlier), with a text from Genesis: "Ye Shall Be as Gods Knowing Good and Evil." The scientist is represented as offering the choice of beneficent and maleficent gases from the jars, around which the Dogs of War lurk. Below, a diplomat and Army and Navy officers ponder the choice.

117

118

118   One of President Compton's important decisions was to appoint Vannevar Bush (left) vice-president and dean of engineering in 1932. The portrait is of George Eastman.

119   George R. Harrison was among the brilliant physicists recruited by President Compton. As director of the Spectroscopy Laboratory, he perfected a ruling engine for making diffraction gratings of unprecedented size and accuracy. He later served as dean of the School of Science for twenty-one years.

119

Harrison had been working in the same general area as Compton: in the use of spectroscopy to study the interaction of electrons and atoms, a burgeoning field of science. They immediately got work started on a new Spectroscopy Laboratory, a small building but meticulously insulated against vibration with a three-foot foundation consisting of layers of sand, felt, transite board, ground cork, and reinforced concrete. It was ready in 1931.

To house physics and chemistry activities, Compton also started construction of the Eastman Laboratories, filling in the gap on the east side of the main M.I.T. complex. When completed in 1932 it was connected through a basement passage with the Spectroscopy Laboratory.

While still at Princeton, Compton had accepted as a graduate student Robert J. Van de Graaff, who, during the previous year as a Rhodes Scholar at Oxford, had developed the design of a new kind of electrostatic generator. Compton brought him along to M.I.T. and construction was started in the dirigible dock at Round Hill on a huge Van de Graaff machine, a type of

120

120   This is the first big Van de Graaff generator, built in the dirigible dock at Round Hill. It was later moved to the campus and, when obsolete, to the Museum of Science.

121   John G. Trump '33 worked with Van de Graaff in designing electrostatic generators that were more efficient and useful than the first monster, though less spectacular. This one produced 1,250,000 volts and was designed to emit X rays for treatment of malignant diseases, a program that continues in the High Voltage Laboratory.

122   Francis Bitter was one of the creative scientists whom President Compton brought to M.I.T. He is shown in 1936 with a magnet that he devised capable of producing a field 150,000 times that of the earth. It used so much power that it was first tried out at the Cambridge Electric Company power plant. Bitter worked with the group in the establishment of the National Magnet Laboratory, which was named for him.

121

122

accelerator that would appear in many versions, for use in medicine and industry as well as in physics research.

Compton was determined not to give up his own research activity, and during his first year at M.I.T. he supervised four graduate students, but he succeeded in spending only one afternoon in the laboratory — and that cut short by a call from his office. Administrative duties were pressing from all sides.

A redistribution of responsibilities was one thing that M.I.T. needed. The new president established three schools as administrative corrals for the departments. Vannevar Bush, heir presumptive to Dugald Jackson in electrical engineering, was made dean of the School of Engineering and vice-president of the Institute. Samuel C. Prescott '94, head of biology, became dean of the School of Science. The Department of Architecture was established as a school with William Emerson as dean. Harry M. Goodwin, dean of graduate students, was appointed dean of a Graduate School (then as now an administrative unit rather than an academic fief). A Division of Humanities was organized to advance what Compton saw as needed strength in that field. And Carroll L. Wilson '32 was chosen as assistant to the president, the first in a line of promising young graduates to be given such responsibility.

The effect of the Depression was being painfully felt. Income from endowment dropped so sharply that near the end of 1932, M.I.T. had to withhold 10 percent of salaries above $500, to be placed in reserve. After two years, however, the Institute was able to distribute the fund.

In the attempt to make ends meet, tuition was increased from $400 to $500. Student enrollment dropped from 2,640 to 2,000. Many students were hard put to pay tuition and were helped by a $1.5 million loan fund that Gerard Swope and other alumni had established just before Compton took office.

The fact that times were tough apparently had a salutary effect on student effort. In the spring term of 1933 the percentage of students qualifying for the Dean's List and the scholastic average for the entire student body were the highest in history. And this was not because M.I.T. was getting easier. Scholarship was being taken more seriously than ever.

Setting an example, as a scientist of achievement, as a man of integrity and humanity, as a friend of everyone, was as important as any other accomplishment of President Compton. Long afterward, Julius Stratton would say:

Dr. Compton was a wise and skillful administrator, but it was no simple art of administration that brought M.I.T. into the small company of great universities. In every sense he was a leader, matching a fine mind with a radiant personality. As one looks back over the years of his presidency, it is easy to discern the tangible, material progress of the Institute; but the great gift that he bestowed upon us was his spirit, the shining example of his own life. We were moved by the transparent honesty of his aims. We felt the warmth of his interests in each and every one of us. . . .

Vannevar Bush was proving to be a great administrator too, complementing in his brusqueness the serenity of Compton in dealing with problems. Not surprisingly, his reputation made him attractive elsewhere, and in 1938 he was offered the presidency of the Carnegie Institution of Washington. The prospect of his leaving M.I.T. was so alarming that Compton proposed asking the Corporation to make Bush president and himself chairman. Bush decided, however, to go to Carnegie — a decision with important consequences.

Back in 1917, during his first year on the Princeton faculty, Compton was asked by Robert A. Millikan, who had just completed the physics research that would win him a Nobel Prize but who was then a major in the Signal Corps, to go to Europe for the National Research Council to gather scientific information useful in military research. He wrote to his parents: "I imagine it will be the most important work that I shall ever get a chance at." Compton underestimated his future.

In 1933, Compton was appointed by President Roosevelt as chairman of a Science Advisory Board, organized to search for ways to combat the Depression. The board survived only two years, but it brought about a reorganization of the patent system, conducted studies that introduced the soil-conservation program, and set a precedent for the service of this kind of agency.

In 1939, as prospects appeared for American involvement in a world conflict, Vannevar Bush began meeting with a small group to discuss what should be done to save the nation from fighting with an obsolete technology. In the group were President Compton, President James B. Conant of Harvard, Frank B. Jewett, who was then president of the National Academy of Sciences, and Richard C. Tolman, dean of the graduate school at Caltech, who had graduated from M.I.T. in 1903 and had been a professor of chemistry there.

Bush was chairman of the National Advisory Committee for Aeronautics, charged with advising the Army and Navy on research, and was the logical man to take the lead. He went to President Roosevelt with a plan formulated by the group for a National Defense Research Committee, received immediate authorization for its establishment, and was appointed chairman.

Although he was Bush's former boss, Compton accepted his leadership without hesitation. In the organization of NDRC he was appointed chairman of Division D, which would be concerned with detection problems, controls, and instruments. He chose four section leaders: detection, Alfred L. Loomis, a member of the M.I.T. Corporation, a financier, and an amateur physicist of distinction; controls, Warren Weaver, director of natural sciences for the Rockefeller Foundation; instruments, George R. Harrison; and heat radiation, Alan C. Bemis '30, a research associate in meteorology at M.I.T.

This was just the beginning. NDRC would beget OSRD and launch the most vast scientific and technological enterprise that the world has ever seen. Karl Compton would travel hundreds of thousands of miles and would be the first U.S. civilian on the devastated streets of Tokyo. During the war he would be able to spend little time at M.I.T. Fortunately, with remarkable perception, he had chosen James R. Killian Jr. as executive assistant to the president. In that position, and then as executive vice-president, Killian assumed enormous responsibilities.

20

M.I.T. Goes to War

The Germans marched into Paris on June 14, 1940, and the next day President Roosevelt signed the document officially establishing NDRC with Vannevar Bush as its head. Although the air blitz of England would not start until September, the threat of invasion was now real. President Compton's assignment of solving "detection" problems was urgent.

Detection mainly meant radar, which was far from perfected. The U.S. Navy had started using radar on its ships in 1939 and the British had an operational system, but performance left much to be desired. Research at Round Hill by Julius Stratton, Edward Bowles, and others had led to a better understanding of microwaves and Alfred Loomis sponsored further research in the private laboratory on his estate at Tuxedo Park, New York, in the summer of 1940.

The Microwave Committee, as Compton's section headed by Loomis and with Bowles as secretary was generally called, found that the chief obstacle to developing better radar was the lack of a sufficiently powerful tube for generating microwaves. The solution came in September, when a British mission headed by Sir Henry Tizard arrived with a black metal trunk filled with secret documents and devices including the resonant cavity magnetron — "the most valuable cargo ever brought to our shores," as it has been described. The magnetron could produce 10-centimeter microwaves at thousands of times the power of the Klystron, which the Loomis researchers were using. Britain's facilities were strained to the breaking point and she needed American help in manufacturing magnetrons and developing radar.

The magnetron was shown to the Microwave Committee at Tuxedo Park and, with Compton, members agreed to establish a laboratory for the all-out development of radar. As a disguise, the name Radiation Laboratory was chosen at the suggestion of a member of the committee, Ernest O. Lawrence, director of the Radiation Laboratory at Berkeley. "Radiation" meant nuclear physics and no one would suspect nuclear physicists of being engaged in anything as practical as military research. (The irony of that view was later to be evident.)

123

123   When they came to M.I.T. for the Mid-Century Convocation in 1949, Alfred Loomis, Sir Henry Tizard, and Lee A. DuBridge (left to right) took another look at the resonant cavity magnetron that made the development of radar possible.

The committee decided the laboratory should be at M.I.T., partly because of the Institute's competence in microwave research. Compton telephoned Jim Killian and asked if he could find 15,000 square feet of space. Killian decided he could by preempting a section of the Steam Laboratory.

The first scientist hired by the Radiation Laboratory was Kenneth T. Bainbridge, a Harvard physicist who had graduated from M.I.T. in electrical engineering in 1925. The committee chose as director of the laboratory Lee A. DuBridge, head of the physics department and dean of the Faculty of Arts and Sciences at the University of Rochester.

Tizard returned to England and John Cockroft, who took his place as head of the British mission, brought the precious magnetron to Cambridge. Percy Spencer, Raytheon's technical genius, had bright ideas on how it could be improved and its manufacture simplified.

Bell Telephone Laboratories sent five magnetrons that it had fabricated to M.I.T. and by December radar antennas were mounted on the roof of Building 6. On January 4, 1941, radar was used to "see" buildings across the river in Boston, and by the time the United States went to war eleven months later the Radiation Laboratory had a running start.

The labors of the Rad Lab through five years were so great and its accomplishments so vital than no summary can do them justice. The laboratory grew until it occupied fifteen acres of floor space in Cambridge and it had

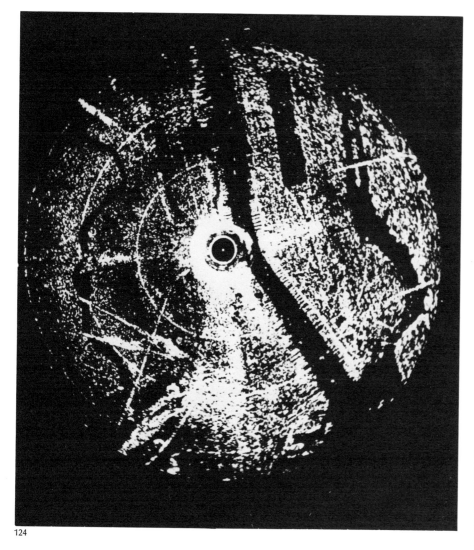

124

124   This view of New York City from 4,000 feet was the kind of picture that Radiation Laboratory radar was giving bombers in 1944. The dark band just to the right of center is the Hudson River. The dark rectangle is Central Park.

stations in many parts of the world. The staff totaled four thousand, including one-fifth of the nation's leading physicists. Four would later receive Nobel Prizes: I. I. Rabi of Columbia, Edward M. Purcell and Julian Schwinger of Harvard, and Luis W. Alvarez of the University of California.

The laboratory developed 150 systems, specialized for almost every conceivable use — detecting airplanes and submarines, blind bombing, gun laying, navigation, and so on. Its operations were second in size only to those for the development of the atomic bomb. And, as has often been said, while the bomb ended the war, radar won it.

Although research was the Rad Lab's job, it could and did produce operating equipment and it organized the Research Construction Company to build prototypes. For example, the H2X airborne radar, which operated with great precision, was developed by 1943 and was scheduled to be manufactured in large quantities by Western Electric and Philco. But the Air Force needed it at once. In a crash program under George E. Valley Jr. '35, a dozen sets were constructed and installed in Flying Fortresses. Crews were sent to Boston and flew the bombers over New England for training in radar. Then they flew to England and for more than four months guided bomber fleets in raids over Germany, at a time when weather seldom permitted visual bombing. By 1944, radar sets began to come from the manufacturers.

LORAN (for Long Range Navigation) came out of the Radiation Laboratory, though it was not a radar system. It provided a grid of radio signals for use by ships and airplanes in determining their location. By the end of the war there were seventy LORAN stations, covering 30 percent of the globe.

Julius Stratton, first attached to the Theory Group in the Radiation Laboratory, then worked on the development of LORAN. When the radio communications system used in ferrying airplanes to Europe proved unsatisfactory, he went to Labrador, Greenland, and Iceland and found it could be improved by using a very low frequency.

Edward Bowles left the Microwave Committee in the spring of 1942 to become special consultant to Secretary of War Henry L. Stimson, who was extremely enthusiastic about radar. Stratton also became a special consultant and traveled to North Africa, Italy, and England in pursuing his duties.

The Office of Scientific Research and Development was organized in early 1941, with Vannevar Bush as its director, and Conant became chairman of NDRC, with Dean Moreland as his executive officer. Compton continued to give special attention to radar but he had many other responsibilities, research on fire control being one. Harold L. Hazen was appointed chief of the Fire Control Division.

It was inevitable that M.I.T. would have leadership in the fire control program, for it had pioneered in servomechanisms, devices using feedback principles in the control of larger devices. Servos had been used in the Integraphs and papers written by Hazen laid the foundation for their development.

At Hazen's request, Gordon Brown had taught a special course for Navy officers in 1939 in the use of servos for fire control, and out of this work came the formation of the Servomechanisms Laboratory, directed by Brown.

This laboratory had important interaction with Charles Stark Draper, professor of aeronautics, who was applying the gyroscope to a new kind of gunsight. The sinking of British warships had demonstrated that the old method of antiaircraft fire, by simple sighting and firing tracer bullets, was totally inadequate. "Doc" Draper devised a "shoebox" sight in which the precessing of gyros would automatically compute the lead needed to shoot down fast-moving dive bombers, torpedo planes, and, later, kamikazes.

The Draper shoebox was mated to a servo drive developed by the Servomechanisms Laboratory for a demonstration of control of a 37mm gun with live ammunition at Fort Heath in Winthrop in June of 1941. The demonstration was impressive. Gordon Brown recalls that an Army representative exclaimed: "Do you see what I see? Why that goddamn little thing on that

125

125 The V-Beam radar, shown on the testing ground in Florida, was one of the most versatile systems developed by the Rad Lab, able to do anything from early warning to ground control. The prototype was built on the rotating mechanism of a carnival merry-go-round. Jim Killian had a hard time convincing military procurement officers that the purchase of a merry-go-round by the Radiation Laboratory was justified.

pipe stand is controlling that great big gun over there!" Further work in Draper's Confidential Instruments Laboratory led to more sophisticated gun-sights and gun directors, and 80,000 of them were in use by the end of 1943. The Servomechanisms Laboratory executed some fifty projects and the Army alone built 30,000 of its controls for guns.

Kenneth Bainbridge in the Radiation Laboratory needed a servocontrol for a new radar to be used on aircraft carriers. The first hand-built model was mounted on the mast of the new *Lexington,* and when it developed bugs, Jay W. Forrester '45, who was on the Servomechanisms Lab staff, was flown to Hawaii as a troubleshooter. While the ship was at sea, he spent a night at the top of the mast making repairs — without a light. He was still aboard when the carrier was torpedoed off Kwajalein, but he returned to Cambridge, unhurt.

Hundreds of other M.I.T. people were at work on various research projects. Philip M. Morse, professor of physics, was a key figure in one of the most consequential fields — Operations Research, developed to apply statistical methods and probability mathematics to tactical and strategic problems. The M.I.T. cyclotron provided radioactive tracers for research in metallurgy, medicine, and chemical warfare. Chemical engineers worked on a variety of problems — fuels, incendiaries, and hydraulic fluids, for instance. The High Voltage Laboratory built five big X-ray machines for use by the Navy in examining munitions (including unexploded shells that were captured). Frederick Keyes and Samuel Collins developed the technology of oxygen production.

In 1943, Karl Compton had been asked to establish an Office of Field Service for the OSRD, cutting across the operations of all its numerous branches. Of the many OFS activities, perhaps the most dramatic was ALSOS, a project headed by Samuel A. Goudsmit from the Radiation Laboratory, to comb Europe for evidence of German research toward an atomic bomb. (The evidence found was largely negative, but this in itself was useful information.) OFS sought to foster good working relationships between scientists and the military in the Pacific Theater, where liaison proved more of a problem than it had in Europe.

126   The staff of the Radiation Laboratory gathered in the Great Court on August 14, 1945, to celebrate a victory and hear about plans for closing the laboratory.

Compton made a survey of the problems in the far-flung commands of the Pacific; soon afterward George R. Harrison was appointed assistant chief of OFS and then went to Australia, where he became chief of the research section of the Southwest Pacific headquarters. John E. Burchard '23, also an assistant chief of OFS, helped set up an Operations Research Section for the Pacific Ocean Areas and later was deputy chief. Moreland resigned as executive officer of NDRC to be chief of the Scientific and Technical Advisory Section at General MacArthur's headquarters. And a Pacific Branch of OSRD was organized, with Compton as director.

Compton and Moreland flew to Manila on the same airplane, arriving on August 5, 1945, the day before the first atomic bomb was dropped on Hiroshima and nine days before Japan's surrender. They went on to Japan to participate in the Scientific Intelligence Survey and thus Compton found himself riding through Tokyo in a jeep, the first American civilian to be seen by the Japanese since before the war.

M.I.T.'s educational program went through drastic changes during the war. Enrollment of regular students dropped from more than 3,000 in 1939 to a low of 1,165 in the spring of 1944. The number of students in the Navy V-12, the Radar School, and other special programs reached a high of 3,629. Alumni in the Armed Forces totaled 8,776 (nearly a fourth of all living alumni), including 98 generals and 52 admirals. Of the total, 148 lost their lives.

M.I.T. had worked under 75 OSRD contracts with a total value of $117,000,000, well above that for any other contractor in the nation. All of the contracts were on a no-gain, no-loss basis. Killian and Nathaniel M. Sage '13, director of the Division of Industrial Cooperation, pioneered in working out this type of contract, which set a pattern for other universities. Review at the end of the war showed that in dollar terms there had been a substantial net loss for the Institute. The impact of the war in intangible ways would be more difficult to assess, but M.I.T. would never be the same again.

M.I.T. did not play a central role in the century's most awesome technological drama but its people were among the stage managers and stagehands.

In their early discussions, Vannevar Bush, Karl Compton, James Conant, Frank Jewett, and Richard Tolman "pondered the possibility of an A-bomb, in Nazi hands or in ours," Bush wrote later. ". . . Although we hardly grasped the revolutionary possibilities at the time, the threat of a possible atomic bomb was in all our minds, and time might well determine whether it became ours or a means for our enslavement."

Among others involved in preliminary studies for the nuclear venture were Professors Warren K. Lewis and John C. Slater and such alumni as William D. Coolidge '96, Robert S. Mulliken '17, Eger V. Murphree '23, and Percival C. Keith Jr. '22. When Bush asked for an officer to represent the Army in planning, Brigadier General Wilhelm D. Styer '22 was assigned. When Manhattan District was formed by the Corps of Engineers to take over the whole program, General Styer selected Brigadier General Leslie R. Groves '17 as the head.

Meanwhile, Arthur Compton's Metallurgical Project staff was building an atomic pile in a squash court at the University of Chicago to determine whether a chain reaction could be achieved. For this he needed sixty tons of uranium. The principal use of uranium up to that time was in glazing pottery, and little of it was available. One of the sources was Metal Hydrides, Inc., of Beverly, Massachusetts, whose president was Peter P. Alexander '33. The uranium powder that it had in stock was a toxic substance with the nasty habit of bursting into flame.

John Chipman, professor of metallurgy, was asked to devise a way to make castings from the powder and to produce several hundred pounds a day for the Chicago pile. He and Albert R. Kaufmann '38, an associate professor, set up a foundry in the old red brick Hood ice cream factory, which stood where the High Voltage Laboratory is now situated.

"No one knew very much about uranium," Chipman recalls. "For example, the International Critical Tables showed that it melted at 1700° C., yet Al and I found that it melted at 1125° C. After it was cast into ingots, Al began experiments on forging and rolling it into cylindrical slugs, about one inch in diameter and four inches long."

John C. G. Wulff, another professor of metallurgy, was asked by Arthur Compton's group to press uranium powder into ingots. "We arranged to use some of the big testing machines in mechanical engineering as presses," he says. "Every day a barrel of 'Powder X' would arrive from Metal Hydrides and our crew would press it into slugs."

Chipman was asked to go to Chicago as chief of the Metallurgy Section of the Metallurgical Project. He set up shop in an old brewery and spent eighteen months there. Morris Cohen '33, another metallurgy professor, took charge of the Cambridge operation.

21

Nuclear Epoch

127

128

127 The decision to make the atomic bomb was well ahead, but when they met at Berkeley in the spring of 1940 these six were discussing a subject of high import — plans for a big new cyclotron at the University of California. From the left, they are Ernest O. Lawrence, director of the Radiation Laboratory at Berkeley; Arthur H. Compton; Vannevar Bush; James B. Conant; Karl T. Compton; and Alfred L. Loomis. Lawrence devised a way to use the cyclotron's magnet in the separation of Uranium-235 for the bomb.

128 Leslie R. Groves, a major general, studied civil engineering at M.I.T. before he went to West Point. As head of Manhattan District he was in complete charge of history's biggest engineering task.

129

129   John C. G. Wulff, a physicist noted for carefully prepared, attention-holding lectures in metallurgy, took on the job of pressing uranium powder into ingots.

While Arthur Compton and Enrico Fermi were assembling the pile, studies were being made elsewhere of how to produce U-235 and plutonium, the ultimate explosive materials. "Doc" Lewis was appointed chairman of a committee to assess alternative processes. The members included Murphree of Standard Oil Development Company and Roger Williams '14 and Crawford H. Greenewalt '22 of Du Pont.

The committee arrived in Chicago on December 2, 1942, to confer with Compton, who did not disclose to them that on that day the first attempt would be made to achieve a sustained chain reaction in the pile. But he asked Greenewalt to join him in witnessing the fateful experiment since he was the youngest and would have the longest memory of the historic event.

In the desperate effort to obtain uranium, Antoine M. Gaudin, professor of metallurgy at M.I.T., made a crucial contribution. Low-grade ore from the Belgian Congo was available and he devised a method by which the uranium could be concentrated for easier extraction. Then it was discovered that gold mines in South Africa had huge wastepiles of rock containing uranium, though in such tiny amounts that extracting it seemed almost too formidable a task. "Tony" Gaudin solved that problem too.

The premier of South Africa, General Jan Christian Smuts, took a personal interest in Gaudin's work. As a young law student at Cambridge University years before, he had been a close friend of another student from the provinces, Richard Maclaurin. During World War II Smuts visited M.I.T. secretly, lunched with Killian and Gaudin, and sorrowfully looked at the portrait of his old schoolmate.

As Manhattan District operations expanded, many people quietly left M.I.T.; their colleagues could only guess where they had gone. Wilcox P. Overbeck '34 of electrical engineering worked at Chicago, Argonne, Oak

130

130　Lying prone with their faces away from the blast, Vannevar Bush and James B. Conant were illuminated by the blinding light of the first atomic bomb test at Alamogordo.

Ridge, and Hanford. George Scatchard of chemistry was a research chairman at Columbia University.

At the Radiation Laboratory, Kenneth J. Germeshausen '31 invented a hydrogen thyratron for high-speed switching that proved useful to trigger the A-bomb and he was often at the Los Alamos Laboratory. (After the war, that remarkable partnership of M.I.T. alumni, Edgerton, Germeshausen & Grier, would have a prime responsibility for nuclear tests. During the war, Harold E. Edgerton '27 and Herbert E. Grier '33 were developing monster strobes for night photography from the air.)

Also from the Radiation Laboratory, Luis Alvarez, Kenneth T. Bainbridge, I. I. Rabi, Jerome B. Wiesner, and Jerrold R. Zacharias went to Los Alamos. Martin Deutsch '37 went from the Radioactivity Center. Charles A. Thomas '24, of Monsanto Chemical Company, was in charge of plutonium chemistry. Cyril S. Smith '26, Victor F. Weisskopf, and Charles D. Coryell, who would later join the faculty, were engaged in research.

When the time came for the first detonation, Philip Morrison (now a theoretical physicist at M.I.T.) cradled the plutonium core of the bomb beside him in the back seat of a car for the drive to Alamogordo. Bainbridge was in charge of the test. For four hours, while rain and lightning threatened to delay the firing, he and George B. Kistiakowsky of Harvard stood guard at the top of the tower on which the bomb was mounted. Lightning had set off a nonatomic test on the tower a few days before.

At 5:30 A.M. on July 16, 1945, at a distance of 17,000 yards, Bush, Conant, Groves, J. R. Oppenheimer, and others witnessed the greatest man-made explosion the world had ever known — an event that not only promised the end of the war but would profoundly affect the future of the world.

With his own heavy responsibilities, Karl Compton had not been involved with Manhattan District. Arthur Compton explained, "Shortly after Pearl Harbor, communications on technical matters between my brother and myself were officially prohibited, and we respected the barrier." But Karl Compton was asked to share in the responsibility for use of the bomb. He, Bush, Conant, and others were appointed to an Interim Committee, with Secretary of War Stimson as chairman, to advise President Truman. The advice was followed and the first bomb was dropped on Hiroshima on August 6, the second on Nagasaki on August 9.

Postwar struggles over the control of atomic energy, H-bomb development, and Oppenheimer's clearance did not involve M.I.T. directly, although alumni and faculty members were parties to the conflicts. President Compton was chairman of the Joint Chiefs of Staff Evaluation Board on Atomic Tests and some of the professors were observers or participants. Clearly, the Pandora's box of nuclear warfare could not be closed, but aside from military issues, nuclear research had a great impact on science and engineering at M.I.T.

The Department of Chemical Engineering set up a practice school at Oak Ridge and became nursemaid for a new course in nuclear engineering that was organized when Manson Benedict '32 joined the faculty in 1951. Benedict had been in charge of the process design of the gaseous diffusion plant at Oak Ridge during the war. In 1955, Theos J. Thompson, who had been chairman of the design committee for a reactor at Los Alamos, became a professor and took charge of the construction of a reactor at M.I.T.

Until then, the few nuclear reactors that had been built were cautiously located at a distance from urban areas. M.I.T.'s was meticulously planned so that it could be located, with safety, adjacent to the campus. It went critical in the summer of 1958 and the Department of Nuclear Engineering was established, with Benedict as its head.

M.I.T. became the leading university in terms of its output of research and nuclear engineers, and safety of reactors was one of the most important subjects of its studies. Thompson was chairman of the Atomic Energy Commission's Advisory Committee on Reactor Safeguards and senior author of a definitive, two-volume work on the subject. He went on leave in 1969 to serve as an AEC commissioner and was killed the next year in an airplane crash near the AEC test site in Nevada.

Another professor, Norman C. Rasmussen '56, spent two years directing a special study for the AEC on reactor safety, a subject of increasing importance and continuing controversy. With 55 American power reactors in operation and 200 set as a national goal for 1985 to help solve the energy crisis, nuclear technology and the training of engineers were critical matters.

When Benedict retired as head of the department in 1971, he was succeeded by Edward A. Mason '48. Mason had served as vice-chairman of the AEC Safeguards Committee, and when the AEC was replaced by two new

131

131   Theos J. Thompson, who designed and directed the M.I.T. Reactor, was the last man to descend into the reactor before the core was installed. He photographed every inch of the interior in order to have a record in case any flaw developed. None did.

132   After it started operating, the reactor was surrounded by experimental apparatus with access through ports to neutron beams.

132

agencies, he was called from M.I.T. to be member of one, the Nuclear Regulatory Commission. The other, the Energy Research and Development Administration, was headed by a former M.I.T. professor, Robert C. Seamans Jr. '42. Rasmussen was appointed head of the department at M.I.T. in 1975.

The M.I.T. reactor was shut down for a year for its first major renovation to increase the neutron intensity of its beam, and when it resumed operating in 1975 it had a busy future ahead. Not only would it be used in the education of 125 graduate students, but for the first time an undergraduate program was started.

P resident Compton was still in the Pacific when he wrote his annual report for 1945. Looking back over the World War II period, he observed: "In these five years the Institute spent on its war contracts as much money as it had spent on its normal activities during its previous 80 years of existence. This is a sobering thought; it makes one wonder what tremendous things could be accomplished in peacetime if the same energy, determination, and resources were marshalled to fashion a better world."

Others were thinking along the same lines. In Washington, Vannevar Bush led in shaping policies for strong government support of peacetime research. The military services were convinced of the value of basic as well as applied science. Researchers — especially physicists — had discovered how much could be accomplished in collaborative effort with ample funding.

Julius Stratton remembers that as early as 1943 there was speculation about "a peacetime sequel" to the Radiation Laboratory. In 1944, he met with Karl Compton, George Harrison (who was then dean of science), Harold Hazen, and John Slater to discuss the possibility of a new kind of laboratory. Slater suggested the name: Research Laboratory of Electronics.

As the Radiation Laboratory approached termination, NDRC established a Basic Research Division, with Stratton as director, to maintain a continuity of fundamental studies and to transfer a treasure of apparatus. In mid-1946, Stratton became director of the new Research Laboratory of Electronics, with headquarters in Building 20, one of the sprawling frame buildings that had been hastily erected for the Rad Lab. Albert G. Hill, who had been a division head at RL, was associate director and then director when Stratton was appointed provost of M.I.T. three years later. Jerome B. Wiesner was Hill's associate and succeeded him as director in 1952, serving through the following nine years. Henry J. Zimmermann '42, Wiesner's associate, succeeded him in 1961.

22

A Postwar Pattern

133

133   Julius A. Stratton, Albert G. Hill, and Jerome B. Wiesner, each of whom was director of the Research Laboratory of Electronics, pictured in about 1949 when Stratton became provost.

The RLE provided a pattern for a number of interdepartmental laboratories and centers. In the words of Stratton, "They take account of the fact that newly emerging fields of science commonly cut across conventional disciplinary lines. And they afford a common meeting ground for science and engineering, for the pure and applied aspects of basic research, to the advantage of both. Perhaps more than any other development in recent years they have contributed to the special character and environment of M.I.T."

Research on plasma provides a good illustration of the RLE approach, especially since it dates to the beginning of the laboratory. The first leader in the program was William P. Allis '23, a physicist who, unlike most scientists, was commissioned by the Army and served the War Department in liaison with NDRC. (He went to Italy in the first ALSOS search for evidence of enemy scientific activity.) Returning after the war, he found that the Radiation Laboratory had sharpened microwave and other tools for research in the area that had chiefly interested him. With Sanborn C. Brown '44 and others, he formed a group for the study of plasmas — ionized gases sometimes described as constituting the fourth state of matter (solid, liquid, and gaseous being the others).

As the H-bomb was being developed, U.S. research was also directed toward achieving controlled thermonuclear fusion, a very attractive goal since it could provide virtually unlimited power for the world. Theoretically, fusion could be attained in an extremely hot plasma. The Atomic Energy Commission, which was conducting secret research toward this end under the name of Project Sherwood, asked RLE to undertake a large classified research program in plasmas. Allis and M.I.T. declined. They believed that

134

134   Benjamin Lax (left) as a graduate student when he and Professor Sanborn C. Brown were photographed at RLE in the late forties while studying gas discharges in a magnetic field.

135   Jerrold R. Zacharias (right) pioneered in molecular beam research at RLE and out of his work came the invention of the atomic clock, used throughout the world for the extremely precise measurement of time. In the foreground is John McClean, technician, and at the left, Nigel Darragh, a student.

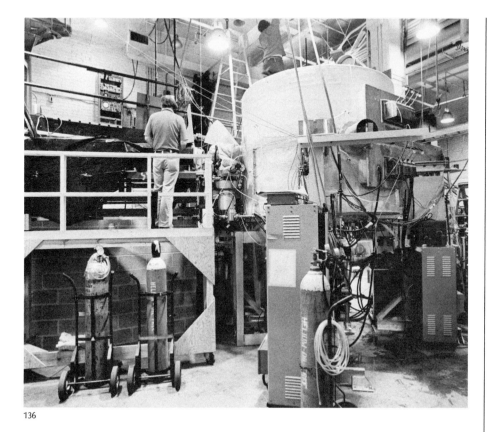

136

136   This is ALCATOR, the machine developed by RLE and the Bitter National Magnet Laboratory as one step (it is hoped) toward controlled fusion. Within the white insulating jacket is the doughnut-shaped chamber in which plasma at an extremely high temperature will be contained by a magnetic field.

plasma research had a long, long way to go before controlled fusion would be feasible and that the field needed more, instead of less, interchange of information among scientists.

The M.I.T. attitude proved to be right and eventually most AEC research was declassified. Exchange of information with Russian scientists began seventeen years ago and controlled fusion is still a distant goal. But knowledge gained from Russian research and elsewhere was used in building ALCATOR, an experimental thermonuclear machine, in collaboration with RLE at the Francis Bitter National Magnet Laboratory.

The Magnet Laboratory is another and impressive example of interdisciplinary effort. Bitter, one of the physicists attracted to M.I.T. by Compton, developed a type of magnet, cooled by water, with which fields of unprecedented power could be attained. He collaborated with the Solid State Physics Division of Lincoln Laboratory, headed by Benjamin Lax '49, in research of such significance that the Magnet Laboratory was formed in 1960. Lax, who had earned his doctorate with plasma research at RLE, became the director. Since the fusion reaction must be contained in a high magnetic field, the Magnet Laboratory provided the ideal facility at which physicists, nuclear engineers, electrical engineers, and others could pursue it.

The advantages of interdisciplinary effort in attacking large problems were sought in the establishment in 1972 of the Energy Laboratory to look for solutions to the world's alarming energy crises. David C. White, Ford Professor of Engineering, was appointed director of a program in which sixty-five professors from ten departments and a large number of graduate students participate. Researchers are examining existing energy technology with the hope of making it more efficient. They are hunting for ways to make new sources of energy, such as solar power and magnetohydrodynamics, of widespread use. Energy crises may be the greatest challenges to technology during the last quarter of the twentieth century. The search for means to meet them will have high priority at M.I.T.

137   A solar energy collector on top of the Citicorp Center, a 56-story building to be erected in New York, was the subject of a study by the M.I.T. Energy Laboratory. The purpose of the study was to determine whether the collector, with an area of one-half acre, could be used to save fuel by operating the dehumidifier in the building's air-conditioning system.

137

When World War II ended, physicists knew they were in an entirely new ball game. Only a decade before, some scientists believed that exploration of the atom was almost over. Wartime research in nuclear physics showed that it was just getting started. There was a rush to put together new teams.

Jerrold R. Zacharias, who had been a student under Rabi at Columbia, was one of the first nuclear physicists recruited from Los Alamos, and he was instrumental in signing up others. Also from Los Alamos came Victor Weisskopf, Bruno B. Rossi, and Bernard T. Feld. Such promising young alumni as Martin Deutsch '37 and Herman Feshbach '42 returned from wartime duties.

A Laboratory for Nuclear Science and Engineering, with Zacharias as director, was organized to bring together talent from various departments. It gave some attention to atomic energy but its people were primarily interested in science and eventually "Engineering" was dropped from the name.

Nuclear physics needed big machines. The cyclotron was modified for research on deuteron-proton reactions. A synchrotron and a linear accelerator were built. The Office of Naval Research provided funds for the ONR Generator, a Van de Graaff machine that was a workhorse for years in producing data on nuclei, chiefly under the direction of William T. Buechner '35, who had been one of Van de Graaff's students.

It was clear, however, that neither M.I.T. nor any other single university could build the biggest machines. Zacharias and friends at other eastern campuses promoted the founding of Brookhaven National Laboratory on Long Island, operated by M.I.T. and eight other members of Associated

23

The Physicists

138   This is the business end of the 600-foot linear accelerator where the 400,000,000 electron-volt beam emerges. It went into operation under the direction of Peter T. Demos in 1974 and was named in memory of Congressman William H. Bates.

138

139

139   This is what a physics doctoral thesis defense looks like. The candidate, in 1968, was William E. Rudge, in shirtsleeves. At the right is George F. Koster '48, a professor. At the left is John C. Slater and, with his back to the camera, Peter D. DeCicco '65, then a young teacher. After Slater was brought to the Institute by President Compton, he was head of the Department of Physics for 21 years. His theoretical work is given much of the credit for the development of radar and he is regarded as one of the world's greatest solid state physicists. The centipede is unexplained.

Universities, Inc., under contract with the Atomic Energy Commission. Philip M. Morse of M.I.T. was the first director and M. Stanley Livingston was the leader in design of the three-billion electron-volt Cosmotron, the largest proton accelerator up to that time.

Livingston was also principal designer of the six-billion electron-volt Cambridge Electron Accelerator, which M.I.T. and Harvard teamed up to build. As a graduate student at Berkeley he had worked under E. O. Lawrence in building the first cyclotron and, appropriately, he climaxed his career by working on the biggest machine to date, the 400-billion volt National Accelerator at Batavia, Illinois.

One by one, the M.I.T. machines were retired and efforts were concentrated on the construction of a 400-million volt linear accelerator at Middleton, Massachusetts, under the direction of Peter T. Demos '51, who had been director of LNS. Though not in a class with the most powerful machines, it was designed to produce a beam of electrons of high intensity and extreme precision.

The time had come, however, when M.I.T. researchers could work at virtually any of the facilities in Europe and the United States. It was at Brookhaven, using the Alternate Gradient Synchrotron, that an M.I.T. group headed by Samuel C. C. Ting discovered a new particle, the J-particle, in 1974. Simultaneously, a group at the Stanford Linear Accelerator produced the same particle. (The choice of the name "J" is a typically subtle joke of physicists. Ting is Chinese and the letter J resembles the Chinese symbol for "ting.")

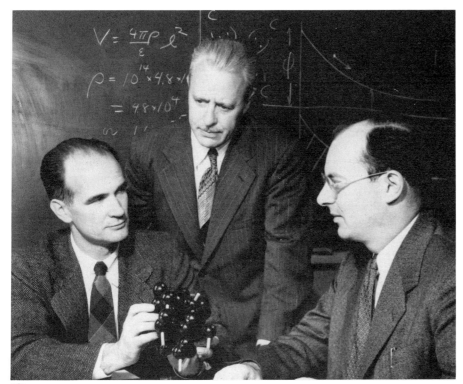

140

141

142

140 William Shockley (left), who did his Ph.D. thesis under Slater in 1936, was the first M.I.T. alumnus to receive the Nobel Prize. He shared it in 1956 with his Bell Laboratories colleagues Walter H. Brattain and John Bardeen for their research in the development of the transistor.

141 Richard P. Feynman, who did his bachelor's thesis under Slater in 1939, shared the Nobel Prize in 1965 with Julian Schwinger of Harvard and a Japanese. A professor of theoretical physics at Caltech for 25 years, he has made particularly important contributions in quantum electrodynamics.

142 Murray Gell-Mann, who earned the Ph.D. at M.I.T. in 1951, won the Nobel Prize in Physics in 1969. He has been at Caltech since 1955. He has worked chiefly on the theory of elementary particles, discovered "strangeness," and suggested the "Eightfold Way" for classification.

The Radioactivity Group was one division of LNS that was extremely productive. Working in this group, Deutsch demonstrated in 1951 for the first time the existence of positronium, an element with a life of one-ten-millionth of a second. The leader of the group, Robley D. Evans, worked for years on the effect of radiation on the human body, and maximum permissible radiation standards — defining the limits of tolerance — were based chiefly on his research. He collected data on hundreds of factory workers who had been poisoned while painting luminous watch dials and victims of medical nostrums made with radium.

A new sector in physics was opened in 1961 with the arrival of Charles H. Townes to serve as provost. At Columbia University he had invented the optical maser, or laser, an achievement for which he received the Nobel Prize in 1964 (sharing it with two Russians). His former student, Ali Javan, who at Bell Telephone Laboratories had invented the gaseous, or continuous-wave, laser, also came to the M.I.T. faculty. Townes resigned to go to the University of California but Javan remained and in the Spectroscopy Laboratory applied laser technology to fundamental research of a high order.

One of M.I.T.'s most famous physics teachers, Hans Mueller, used to startle classes by demanding whether, in the same way that a radio antenna receives radio waves, an antenna could receive light waves. The answer was no, that the antenna would have to be smaller than the light waves, and to make one seemed impossible.

But Ali Javan succeeded in making such an antenna, a tungsten wire with a tip only about one-fourth of a millionth of an inch in diameter, for use in laser experiments enabling him to measure the speed of light with a precision never attained before.

143   Ali Javan (left) and Charles H. Townes used lasers to check on one consequence of the Special Theory of Relativity, working in a wine cellar at Round Hill because of its freedom from vibrations. While at M.I.T., Townes shared the Nobel Prize in 1964 for his invention of the laser. Javan, his former student, invented the gaseous laser.

144

145

144   Hans Mueller was one of M.I.T.'s greatest teachers, explaining difficult concepts in physics with demonstrations and dramatic lectures. He did important research on the passage of light through matter.

145   Victor F. Weisskopf, a theoretical physicist of distinction, is regarded as one of the world's leading statesmen of science.

Behind all experimental physics, and making use of the data produced by experiments, is theory. As experimentalists advanced into new realms, the work of theoreticians had become increasingly important and difficult. In 1968 a Center for Theoretical Physics was established, not simply an administrative unit but an environment conducive to thinking and exchanging ideas, with quiet rooms and an abundance of blackboards. The group there has recently developed the Bag Theory, which in a simple, classical way put subnuclear particles in a "bag" and accounts for the fact that free quarks and partons have not been found.

After Weisskopf, a theoretical physicist, retired as head of the Physics Department, physicists from far and wide came to M.I.T. to honor him in the fall of 1974. Feshbach, who had been director of the Center for Theoretical Physics, succeeded him and was succeeded at the center by Francis E. Low, a specialist on the properties of electrons and the origin of mass and charge.

The pace of life at M.I.T. did not slacken after the war but, with the grimness of pressures gone, the Institute could direct its extraordinary vitality to long-deferred needs and new opportunities. President Compton and Vice-President Killian held intensive discussions with the Executive Committee of the Corporation on policies and planning for the new period.

Establishment of the Research Laboratory of Electronics and the Laboratory for Nuclear Science, with the recruiting of top physicists, resulted from such planning. An immediate challenge had to be met — an 80 percent increase in student enrollment over the prewar level, to 5,660. Nearly a third of the returning GIs were married and many had children. They needed living quarters. A hundred frame houses, designed by the Department of Architecture, were erected at the west end of Briggs Field, the first such project in an American college. Two-story Navy barracks were moved from Rhode Island to provide apartments for 180 families.

A number of new buildings were made possible by major gifts, Institute funds, and a campaign, with Marshall B. Dalton '15 as general chairman, which brought in $26,000,000. The Charles Hayden Memorial Library, the Sloan Metals Processing Laboratory, the John Thompson Dorrance Laboratory, Kresge Auditorium and Chapel, and Baker House were the principal new buildings of the period. The Riverside Apartment Hotel was purchased and became Burton House.

24

Bettering the Campsite

147

146

146   In 1946, houses for veterans had been built on the west end of Briggs Field and the land was being prepared (foreground) for Navy barracks for others.

147   The former barracks did not make ideal homes but they enabled many former GIs to live close to M.I.T. The trend toward an increasing number of married students was started.

Killian initiated a comprehensive study of educational policies, methods, goals, and choices that provided a blueprint for the Institute's development in the years ahead. Beginning in 1947 the Committee on Educational Survey, composed of key members of the faculty, spent two years on the study and produced a landmark report, generally known as the Lewis Report because the chairman was Warren K. Lewis. Julius Stratton was mainly responsible for the document that came out of the study.

The committee rejected the idea that professional education in science and engineering should be offered only in graduate programs like those for medicine and law. It observed that "technological and social problems are so inextricably interwoven that the humanities and social sciences are also components of man's professional life" and recommended the establishment of a School of Humanities and Social Studies.

Implementation of the Lewis Report became primarily the responsibility of Killian. In the fall of 1948 he was elected president and Karl Compton, chairman of the Corporation. Compton continued to be in demand for national service. When Vannevar Bush resigned as chairman of the Research and Development Board of the National Military Establishment, Compton agreed to take his place, and that meant spending more time in Washington.

The inauguration of Killian was held on April 2, 1949, as the climax of an intellectual festival of monumental proportions. "Mid-Century Convocation

148   James R. Killian Jr. presented a lectureship to Sir Winston Churchill when he spoke at the Mid-Century Convocation. (M.I.T. has never given an honorary degree and decided not to break with precedent in this case.) Behind Churchill are, left to right, Karl T. Compton, John E. Burchard, and Governor Paul A. Dever.

on the Social Implications of Scientific Progress" was the lofty title for the occasion. The star was the greatest statesman the century had produced — Winston Churchill. Some three dozen other notables, including Vannevar Bush, Nelson A. Rockefeller, Sir Henry Tizard, Sir Richard Livingstone, and Jacques Maritain, participated in symposia on various aspects of the main subject.

Everyone wanted to hear Churchill speak and on short notice the event was moved to Boston Garden, necessitating heroic efforts in revising logistics under the direction of John E. Burchard, recently appointed dean of humanities and impresario for the convocation. Churchill's performance fulfilled expectations. The Cold War was his theme and he declared: "We seek nothing from Russia but good will and fair play. If, however, there is to be a war of nerves let us be sure our nerves are strong and are fortified by the deepest convictions of our hearts."

In his inaugural address two days later, President Killian expressed another concern: "In a period of armed truce, the fundamental principle of academic freedom is subject to stresses which we have not met before. . . . We must hope that the cold war may not diminish the opportunity to be free, either on the part of the educational institution or on the part of the scholar himself."

Killian was not discussing a remote abstraction. Politicians, press, and zealots were just getting warmed up in the hunt for Communists, especially on the campuses. Within a week events led him to issue a classic declaration of policy that would guide M.I.T. through difficult years. In part, it said:

The Institute is unequivocally opposed to Communism; it is also sternly opposed to the Communistic method of dictating to scholars the opinions they must have and the doctrines they must teach. M.I.T. seeks first a faculty and staff of thoroughly competent scholars and teachers of high integrity. Assuming their competence and integrity, it believes that its faculty, as long as its members abide by the law and maintain the dignity and responsibilities of their position, must be free to inquire, to challenge, and to doubt in their search for what is true and good.

The stand demonstrated the mettle and principles of the new president. Son of a South Carolina textile manufacturer and a graduate in management, Killian was temperamentally conservative, but the faculty found he had broad cultural interests, strongly humanist motivation, a boldness in undertaking new ventures, and a wholehearted devotion to M.I.T. Associated with him in the newly created position of provost was Julius Stratton, with great strength in science and engineering and special gifts both personal and administrative.

In the spring of 1949 Karl Compton had to be hospitalized and was unable to attend commencement. He was stricken again in the late summer and resigned as chairman of the Joint Research and Development Board. (He was

149

149   K. T. Compton was a lover of the outdoors. In his handwriting, it is noted that the picture was made at Quartet Camp in Maine.

succeeded by William Webster '23, Boston utilities executive.) He recovered and he and Mrs. Compton, always devoted to the Institute, were active in campus life. Shortly after commencement in 1954, K.T. was in New York when he suffered a heart attack. He died there on June 22.

At a memorial service, President Killian pointed out that Compton had been a lover of the woods, of canoeing and fishing, and said that not long before his death he was asked to summarize his philosophy of life. Dr. Compton had responded: "My wife and I have adopted as a motto a phrase which we saw on a sign at a campsite on one of our canoe trips north of the Minnesota border: 'Leave every campsite better than you found it.' This, we think, is a good guiding principle in any situation in which one's lot happens to be cast."

Commented President Killian: "Karl Compton was superbly successful in leaving every campsite better than he found it."

During the early fifties, Killian's services were increasingly sought in dealing with technological and educational problems on a national level. President Eisenhower, for instance, appointed him chairman of the Technical Capabilities Panel of the President's Science Advisory Committee, known as the Killian Panel, to work on a strategic response to Russian power.

Privy to developments that gave him perspective on major stresses, Killian became a leading spokesman in urging greater effectiveness in technological education. The number of students entering engineering and some fields of science had been declining at a time when Russia was building up its technical manpower.

The situation was dramatized when the Russians launched a Sputnik on October 4, 1957, beating the Americans into space, proving that they were

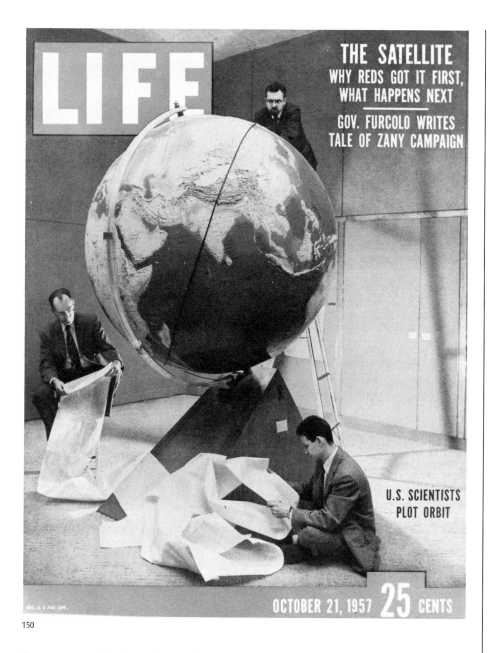

150

150   This cover on *Life* made graphic the consternation that followed Russia's launching of a Sputnik. The Smithsonian Observatory had arranged to use the M.I.T. Computation Laboratory in calculating the orbit of the little 3¼-pound Vanguard that the U.S. was planning to launch. Suddenly they had Sputnik to follow. *Life* posed Fred L. Whipple (left), J. Allen Hynek (top), and Don Lautman of Smithsonian with the M.I.T. Map Room globe.

by no means backward in technology and demonstrating that they had the rocket power to launch intercontinental missiles.

In the crisis, President Eisenhower appointed Killian as his special assistant for science and technology. Julius Stratton, who the year before had been made chancellor, became acting president of M.I.T.

In Washington, Killian provided the cool-headed judiciousness that was needed. Upon his recommendation, the National Advisory Committee for Aeronautics (NACA) was re-formed as the National Aeronautics and Space Administration (NASA) to conduct the civilian space program. He chaired a group that untangled responsibilities for space (Army–Air Force rivalry had been one reason for the American lag) and allocated missions and facilities in the civilian and military programs.

Killian arranged for the President's Science Advisory Committee to report directly to the President rather than to the Office of Defense Mobilization. He was chosen as its chairman and he had direct access to the President. PSAC called on the services of as many as three hundred leading experts to study a wide range of problems. Their recommendations had important consequences, such as the later establishment of the Arms Control and Disarmament Agency and ultimate achievement of a treaty banning nuclear tests in the atmosphere.

151   As President Eisenhower watched, Killian was sworn in by Sherman Adams, assistant to the President. Mrs. Killian was unable to attend the ceremony so his daughter, Carolyn — Mrs. Paul Staley — was with him.

152

152   A third career for James R. Killian Jr. was being "father of public television." He was a leader in the development of WGBH as an educational station for Boston. In 1965 he became chairman of the National Commission on Educational Television, which developed a plan for federal support under a new concept of "public broadcasting." He served for nearly two years as chairman of the Corporation for Public Broadcasting. After he stepped down as chairman he was honored at a "Salute to Killian" dinner given in Washington by the Advisory Council to National Organizations. Children from the cast of *Zoom,* a popular program, were on hand (above) to help thank him.

Never ostentatious, Killian's influence was exerted in many ways. When in 1959 he decided to return to M.I.T., he was succeeded as the President's science adviser by George B. Kistiakowsky of Harvard, who had served under him on PSAC. And another PSAC member of that time, Jerome B. Wiesner of M.I.T., became President Kennedy's science adviser. The White House continued to look to men with Cambridge background. Lee A. DuBridge was science adviser from 1969 to 1970 and Edward E. David Jr. '47 from 1970 to 1973. As director of the National Science Foundation, H. Guyford Stever, a former professor, then had the responsibility.

Reflecting on discussions at the Mid-Century Convocation, President Killian commented in his first annual report: "We need better linkages between science and the humanities, with the object of fusing the two into a broad humanism that rests upon both science and the liberal arts and that does not weaken either. We need bifocal vision to thread our way among the problems of modern society."

There was precedent for this view. One of the Institute's original purposes, as set down by President Rogers in 1865, was "to furnish a general education, founded upon the Mathematical, Physical, and Natural Sciences, English and other Modern Languages, and Mental and Political Science, as shall form a fitting preparation for any of the departments of active life."

President Walker strengthened the social science content of the curriculum but later the field languished. President Compton provided new status by setting up the Division of Humanities, with three departments — economics and social science, English and history, and modern languages.

Circumstances in the late forties were propitious for the School of Humanities and Social Studies. Construction of the Hayden Library would provide a home for it. John E. Burchard, new director of the libraries and appointed dean of humanities in 1948, was a humanist of uncommonly broad interests and a rare capacity for enterprise. A 1923 graduate in architectural engineering, he had taught in both the Architecture and Civil Engineering departments and was deeply interested in the arts and the world of books.

25

Linkages for Humanism

153   John E. Burchard, who, as director of libraries, was the principal planner of Hayden Library, and who became the first dean of the School of Humanities and Social Science.

With limited funds, yet with an aspiration to make humanities and social science pervade the soul of technology, the new school had the problem of building a faculty of scholarly distinction and alluring undergraduates dubious about ideas that can't be reduced to equations. Nevertheless, through Burchard's tenure, that of Robert L. Bishop, an economist who succeeded him in 1964, and that of Harold J. Hanham, a historian from Harvard who became dean in 1973, the school developed in scope and vigor. Departments of Political Science, Psychology, and Philosophy were added.

The Department of Humanities is a school in itself, including programs in history, literature, writing, anthropology, and music as well as Course XXI, the double major for science and engineering students. Its head for more than a decade was Richard M. Douglas, a Renaissance historian, who served during a period of rapid ideological and curricular change. He was succeeded by Bruce Mazlish, the first historian to offer a course in the application of psychoanalysis to history and biography.

A demonstration that M.I.T. is capable of producing a humanist scholar was given by Nathan Sivin '52, one of the first graduates of Course XXI. He studied in Taipei, Singapore, Kyoto, and Leiden, received a doctorate at Harvard, and returned to the Institute, versed in Chinese and Japanese and an expert on the history of Chinese science. He was a leader in organizing Technology Studies, a program involving professors from various disciplines.

Relating humanities to ancient technology, Cyril S. Smith, distinguished metallurgist, applied his knowledge to archaeological studies (the ancient metallurgy of swordmaking, for instance). Heather N. Lechtman, with a background in art, physics, and chemistry, has been studying pre-Columbian metallurgical sites and artifacts — especially gold — in the Andes. Arthur R. Steinberg has studied the ancient technology of Italy and early copper sites in Cyprus.

In literature, a legendary figure comparable to Tubby Rogers, and a greater poet and scholar, was William C. Greene, who retired after forty-one years on the faculty. He used salty language in challenging students to honesty in thinking and they called him "Profanity" Greene. He was a doctor for ailing productions of Tech Show for twenty-five years.

Bill Greene's competence in stagecraft was that of a very sophisticated amateur. For more than twenty years Joseph D. Everingham has brought professionalism to the teaching and production of drama, with the result that M.I.T. is in the vanguard of theater arts. Students have also had the stimulation of Albert R. Gurney Jr., a leading young playwright. ("The best mainstream play to come out of America since the debut of Arthur Miller," said the London *Times* of his *Children*.) Barry Spacks, novelist and poet, is among the teachers who are writers of distinction.

In music, the school has sought teachers who are practitioners as well as scholars. The standard was set with the appointment of Klaus Liepmann, violinist and conductor, and Gregory Tucker, pianist and composer. John Harbison and John Buttrick are outstanding pianists and Harbison is a notable composer. The Symphony Orchestra, directed by David M. Epstein, also a composer, has proved its excellence on national tours. More than a thousand students take the three-dozen music courses and some eight hundred participate in performances by a variety of musical groups.

Changing the name of the Department of Modern Languages to Department of Foreign Literatures and Linguistics indicates the evolution through which it has gone in the past two decades. William N. Locke, who became head of the department in 1945, developed laboratories with playback aids for teaching and fostered interest in the "science of languages," especially in the Research Laboratory of Electronics, beginning with a conference on speech analysis in 1949.

Morris Halle, who was then working at Harvard on his doctorate under Roman Jakobson, the world's most renowned linguist, joined the department in 1951 and collaborated with others at RLE. Interest in the possibilities of machine translation was growing and federal funds became available for research in this direction. An understanding of the structure of language was essential.

Noam A. Chomsky, who had been working on his doctoral dissertation, "Transformational Analysis," while a Junior Fellow at Harvard, joined the department in 1955 and two years later Jakobson accepted a joint appointment at M.I.T.

M.I.T. researchers became disenchanted with machine translation but meanwhile they had developed the foremost center of linguistics. Chomsky devised a revolutionary approach known as transformational grammar, which has profound implications for psychology since it involves a conviction that language is based on an innate structure of the mind.

Linguistics grew out of research achievements. The Department of Psychology, established in 1964, was the product of a plan and began with a search for a distinguished scientist to organize the program. The search produced Hans-Lukas Teuber, who in ten years as head of the department has built a strong, though relatively small, faculty. Richard M. Held has demonstrated that active muscular movement is essential to visual perception. Walle J. H. Nauta, an Institute Professor, has elucidated brain structure and function. Teuber has conducted a unique study of brain damage effects, research that helps in understanding normal brain activity. Beyond his research, his exciting teaching has made his "Introduction to Psychology and Brain Science" the most popular course in the Institute. Practically every student takes it, as many as nine hundred signing up each year for the series of two-hour evening lectures.

A philosophy department was established in 1873 but it fell by the wayside and nearly a century passed before another department was organized. Huston C. Smith for a number of years offered studies in Oriental philosophies and religions. Richard L. Cartwright, present head of the department, has been strengthening ties with linguistics, psychology, and mathematics.

154

156

155

157

158

159

160

154   William C. "Profanity" Greene had a caustic way of challenging students in English literature courses.

155   Klaus Liepmann, violinist and conductor, and Gregory Tucker, pianist, set a high standard for music studies.

156   John Buttrick is a concert pianist as well as an excellent teacher.

157   Albert R. Gurney has written some two dozen plays and a novel, *The Gospel According to Joseph*.

158   Richard M. Douglas, a Renaissance historian, was head of the Department of Humanities for more than a decade.

159   Noam Chomsky, Ferrari P. Ward Professor of Modern Languages and Linguistics, is the leading exponent of transformational grammar.

160   Barry Vercoe, explorer in electronic music, at the keyboard controlling a computer given to M.I.T. by Digital Equipment Corporation founded by Kenneth H. Olsen '50 and represented here by Richard J. Clayton '62 (center). At left is Dean Harold J. Hanham of the School of Humanities and Social Science.

161

161   A young monkey deprived of sight of its limbs can be trained to pull a cord, which will give it a suck on a stick of candy, psychologists found. But learning to do this with one hand is not helpful in trying to do it with the other, untrained hand. The experiment is one of those performed under the direction of Richard Held to study the relationship between muscular movement and perception.

162   Hans-Lukas Teuber, head of the Department of Psychology, reports to the staff on a scientific meeting he had attended.

162

A study of the century's greatest achievements in social science, published by *Science,* included among the innovators eleven who are, or have been, members of the M.I.T. faculty. Three qualified as economists, Paul N. Rosenstein-Rodan, Paul A. Samuelson, and Evsey D. Domar; two as political scientists, Karl W. Deutsch and Ithiel de Sola Pool. The research of the other six had great impact on social science: Roman Jakobson and Noam Chomsky in linguistics, and Vannevar Bush, Samuel H. Caldwell '25, Norbert Wiener, and Claude E. Shannon in computation and information theory.

No claim is made that the list is definitive, but it is interesting to examine, especially because it recognized an interplay between technology and social science, which has been significant at M.I.T.

President Francis A. Walker set a standard for a rigorous, scientific approach to economics. The *Statistical Atlas,* published after the 1870 census that he directed, was acclaimed for its scientific method and graphical excellence. He included manufacturing statistics for the first time in the 1880 census and produced a solid, twenty-two-volume report. He was a founder of the American Economic Association in 1885 and chosen as its first president with the support of the vigorous young Turks.

One of Walker's appointees at M.I.T. was Davis R. Dewey, a respected economist for half a century. When President Compton took office, Dewey was within three years of retirement. A section of his Department of Economics and Statistics was split off as a new Department of Business and Engineering Administration under Erwin H. Schell '12. Ralph E. Freeman became head of economics. Charles A. Myers and W. Rupert Maclaurin were among those who joined the faculty in the following years.

Maclaurin was the son of President Maclaurin. (Another son, Richard Colin Maclaurin, was an administrative officer for thirteen years.) He is credited with recruiting such economists as E. Cary Brown, now head, Robert L. Bishop, former head of the department; Charles P. Kindleberger, Morris A. Adelman, and Paul A. Samuelson.

Samuelson is undoubtedly the most widely read economist in the world, partly because he writes prolifically, lucidly, and even entertainingly. His *Economics* has passed three million in sales. But he was not given the Nobel Prize for popularity. The rigor and originality of his mathematical methods are greatly respected by other economists and his studies have covered an exceptionally broad area, providing, in fact, unifying theory for economics. Robert M. Solow, a close friend and a frequent collaborator with Samuelson, is held in equal esteem by other economists.

M.I.T.'s serious entry into the field of political science was, curiously, related to electronics rather than to eminence in economics — or what had been known in Walker's day as political economy. As the Cold War grew tense, the Department of State asked the Institute what could be done about Soviet jamming of Voice of America broadcasts. The M.I.T. response was that the problem probably was greater than one of electronics, that it concerned all the ways in which information could be transmitted and, in

26

The Social Scientists

163

164

163   Davis R. Dewey, professor of economics from 1886 to 1933. His son, Bradley Dewey '09 was an industrialist and a member of the Corporation for 43 years. Two grandchildren went to M.I.T.: Bradley Dewey Jr. '40 and Davis R. Dewey II '41.

164   Receiving the Nobel Prize from the king of Sweden in 1970, Paul Samuelson was the second economist to win an award.

165   Like Samuelson, his close associate Robert M. Solow is an Institute Professor and highly respected by other economists.

165

fact, the nature of the message. The result was a study in 1950 known as Project Troy.

The director of Project Troy was Dean John E. Burchard and one of the leading participants was Max F. Millikan, who had recently joined the economics faculty. During World War II Millikan had been chief economist in the State Department intelligence branch and for a time he was on the Central Intelligence Agency staff.

Project Troy covered a lot of ground but its most important conclusion, so far as M.I.T. was concerned, was that further research was needed on international communications. The result was the establishment of the Center for International Studies in 1951. Millikan became the director.

Closely allied with Millikan in the center was Walt Whitman Rostow, an economic historian. Their 1957 book, *A Proposal, Key to an Effective Foreign Policy,* urging a comprehensive foreign economic and technical aid program, represented a point of view that would be influential in the years ahead. Rostow's role in President Kennedy's administration and then as chief foreign policy braintruster for President Lyndon Johnson made him a nationally controversial figure. Less well known is the fact that the Peace Corps grew out of Millikan's recommendation.

A researcher at the center who came to national attention for rather different reasons was Daniel Ellsberg, formerly of the Rand Corporation, who made the Pentagon Papers public in 1971.

The Department of Political Science was formed in 1965 with a faculty that has included such luminaries as Norman J. Padelford, William E. Griffith, Everett E. Hagen, Harold R. Isaacs, Daniel Lerner, Lucian W. Pye, and Myron Weiner. Ithiel de Sola Pool pioneered in computer simulation of international relations and public opinion. Lincoln P. Bloomfield initiated research in arms control, a field in which George W. Rathjens also became prominent after service in the U.S. Arms Control and Disarmament Agency. William W. Kaufmann is an authority on national security and defense studies.

The first head of the department was Robert C. Wood, who soon left to serve as under secretary (and briefly as secretary) of the Department of Housing and Urban Development. He returned from Washington to be director of the Joint Center for Urban Studies and then became president of the University of Massachusetts.

Eugene B. Skolnikoff, who graduated from M.I.T. in electrical engineering in 1949 and was a Rhodes Scholar, returned to get a Ph.D. in political science; he became head of the department and later director of the Center for International Studies. Weiner, a specialist in the politics of India and South Asia, succeeded him as department head.

Vannevar Bush was by no means satisfied in the prewar period with the differential analyzer, advanced though it was. In 1937 he wrote a series of memoranda about the possibilities of an electronic Rapid Arithmetical Machine that would be faster and more flexible.

Some preliminary work was done on such a machine. Wilcox P. Overbeck developed new types of tubes for it and estimated he could achieve counting speeds of a million per second. Perry O. Crawford Jr. '39 investigated the possibility of using digital computation, with binary numbers, in gunfire control. They, and others at M.I.T., were diverted by wartime duties from a pursuit of what proved to be an epochal goal.

It was Jay W. Forrester who made the breakthrough — not suddenly but through years of obstinate effort. Captain Luis de Florez '11, director of the Special Devices Division of the Navy Office of Research and Inventions, had proposed the development of an all-purpose flight training machine for pilots. In place of a trainer for each type of aircraft, such a machine could simulate the characteristics of all types.

The project wound up in the Servomechanisms Laboratory in 1944, and Gordon S. Brown, the director, assigned it to Forrester, his assistant. Forrester chose Robert R. Everett '43 to work with him in what proved to be a close partnership, and the team was further expanded.

The project was started with the expectation of applying analog computer techniques such as Bush had used in the differential analyzers. As time went on, however, it became apparent that an analog machine, with rotating rods, could not provide the speed and versatility that was needed. Forrester began thinking about the possibility of using digital computation.

"You can count faster than you can measure" is Brown's succinct summary of the value of the digital method.

The war was over and it was 1946 before Forrester could switch to the digital method in his project. Meanwhile, Harvard had built Mark I, a non-

27

Counting on Machines

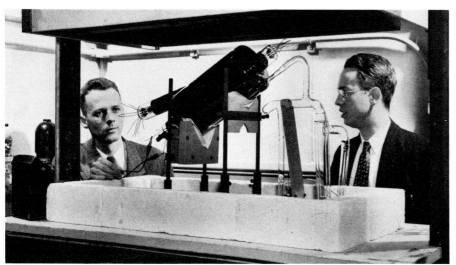

166   Jay W. Forrester (left) built this electrostatic storage tube for Whirlwind's memory but it had a capacity of only 400 digits. Though advanced for that time, this limited the computer's usefulness. At right is Stephen H. Dodd Jr. '42.

electronic but large-scale automatic computer. At the University of Pennsylvania, ENIAC, using vacuum tubes, had been built and EDVAC was under construction. The dropping of wartime secrecy made information about such research available, but the machines had shortcomings.

As time went on, the application of Forrester's machine to a flight trainer was dropped, and the computer itself, now known as Whirlwind, became the object of the undertaking. The vicissitudes through which the project passed, in technical development and funding, were numerous and complex. It doubtless would have expired but for Forrester's persistence, and was at the point of expiring when it was found to be a major solution for a Project Lincoln problem. Not until 1953, after a decade of strenuous effort, did Whirlwind begin to fulfill its purpose as a high-capacity, high-speed, highly reliable computer, "perhaps the most influential of the early computers in terms of today's commercial machines."

In 1957, with generous support from the IBM Corporation, M.I.T. opened a Computation Center (which also served other colleges), the first such campus center in the country. From then on, researchers were chiefly engaged in exploiting the potential for computer use rather than in developing computers, though hardware innovations were made too. Professors and students in every department found that computers could greatly extend their power to deal with research problems and there seemed no end in sight for computer services. The Computation Center expanded its equipment and acquired new computers without satisfying the demand.

One major bottleneck, and a constant source of frustration, was the batch processing system. A user might turn over a set of punched cards to the Computation Center and then wait days for the result — even though the computer might solve the problem in a few seconds. And even then the user might find that an error in his programming would require another run. The answer to this kind of difficulty was time-sharing, developed chiefly by Fernando J. Corbato, a physics graduate of 1956. A computer could be linked to several control consoles and could serve several users so rapidly that for all practical purposes the service was simultaneous. The user could make changes in his program immediately.

This system came into use in 1963. In that same year, Project MAC, supported by the Advanced Research Project Agency of the Department of Defense, was inaugurated. MAC (an acronym for Machine-Aided Cognition and Multiple-Access Computer) carried the time-sharing concept still further, permitting interaction between user and machine to an extent hardly dreamed of in the past. With a staff of 270 people, representing various departments, the MAC laboratory continues to explore new frontiers, giving special attention to methods by which users can talk to computers in "natural" languages and computers can be capable of using some common sense.

To serve the entire M.I.T. community, Information Processing Services was organized and established in its own building in 1968. Nearly as un-

167 The magnetic core memory invented by Forrester, consisting of doughnut-shaped ferrite rings strung on fine wires, solved the memory problems for Whirlwind and made rapid advances possible in computer technology everywhere.

167

obtrusively as the telephone system, it responds through time-sharing to the demands of nearly 400 terminals. Some two-thirds of the Institute's students and faculty use it at some time or other and there are normally about 4,500 active users. IPS has its own programs, called ''daemons,'' that it employs for accounting and housekeeping.

In addition there are about 150 minicomputers and ten computing centers connected with IPS and it has a link with MAC. It is also developing methods of ''networking'' — sharing the workload with computers outside M.I.T., such as those in the ARPA network and at Harvard and other New England colleges. The ubiquitous slide rule that Tech students used to carry has well nigh disappeared. Many of them have pocket calculators.

Jerrold Zacharias once wisecracked, ''M.I.T. has computers like other people have mice.''

168   By 1954, Whirlwind had demonstrated its phenomenal power in Lincoln Laboratory's experimental Cape Cod System, processing as many as 16 digits at a rate of 20,000 times a second. From the left are Jay W. Forrester, Norman H. Taylor '39, ''Gus'' O'Brien, and Norman L. Daggett '47. On the ladder is Charles L. Corderman '50.

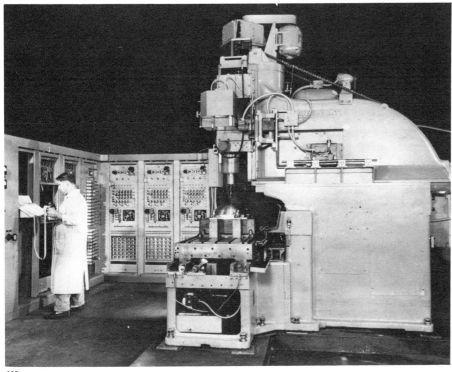

169

169 Numerical control, which revolutionized the machine tool industry, was one of the important accomplishments of the Servomechanisms Laboratory. Research was started in 1949 when Gordon S. Brown was director and completed in 1960 after the name of the laboratory, then under the direction of J. Francis Reintjes, had been changed to Electronic Systems Laboratory.

170 In the Artificial Intelligence Laboratory, Marvin L. Minsky, now Donner Professor of Science in Electrical Engineering, developed a computer-controlled robot, with a television camera for an eye, that could accomplish simple tasks such as stacking blocks. Much greater sophistication has since been attained.

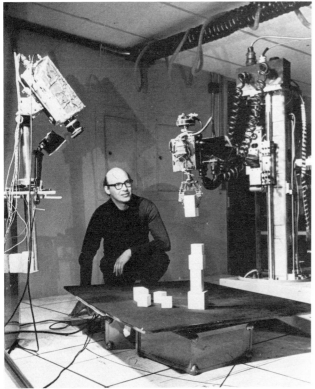

170

Norbert Wiener and Claude Shannon were M.I.T.'s two principal mathematical prestidigitators in the advent of digital computers. The prestige of the Department of Mathematics was built, however, through the accomplishments of a number of professors, especially during the twenty-one years that William Ted Martin was the head.

Isadore M. Singer is one of the most eminent members of the faculty. "Probably no living American mathematician has made basic contributions in so many fields," according to Kenneth M. Hoffman, now the department head. "His great gift is his penetrating insight. It is apparent that only a mathematician with profound insight could approach such varied fields, each time producing work which marks a turning point in the subject."

Another notable was Norman Levinson '33, who had made progress toward proving the famous Riemann Hypothesis, a conjecture with which mathematicians have been struggling for more than a century. And there are other outstanding mathematicians on the teaching staff of eighty — all Ph.D.'s — who include specialists in every major field. The department has the reputation of being one of the five strongest in the country and has the broadest program of any.

Computers have had no impact on the most abstract areas of mathematics, but in others, such as artificial intelligence, they have stimulated new exploration or, as in statistics, served as valuable tools. The need for a mathematical logic in extending the power of computers has increased the enthusiasm of many students for the subject, especially students in electrical engineering.

Claude Shannon, who had graduated from the University of Michigan with degrees in both mathematics and electrical engineering, came to M.I.T. as a graduate student and in 1940 received both a master's degree in electrical engineering and a Ph.D. in mathematics. In a part-time job, he worked on Vannevar Bush's differential analyzer and, because of problems in operating the machine's relay circuits, devised a new approach that he described in his master's thesis and that laid the groundwork for the design of electronic digital computers.

During World War II, Shannon worked at Bell Telephone Laboratories on cryptography and secrecy systems. Treating communications from a statistical point of view, he developed "information theory," which has been invaluable in innumerable ways, from design of the world's telephone switching circuits to industrial automation. He became popularly known for devising a mechanical mouse that could learn how to thread its way through a maze to get a brass cheese (an accomplishment which he would now prefer to forget). Shannon returned to M.I.T. in 1956 and came to hold a professorship in both the Departments of Mathematics and Electrical Engineering.

Shannon was indebted in part to the mathematics of Norbert Wiener, as were other scientists and engineers in many fields. Wiener undoubtedly was the most versatile genius in M.I.T.'s history, celebrated not only for his brilliance but also for quirks and boundless interests. A rotund, goateed man,

28
The
Mathematicians

171 Norbert Wiener had trouble with arithmetic as a fourth-grader in Cambridge and his father, Leo Wiener, a professor of Slavic languages at Harvard, withdrew him from Peabody School to do the teaching himself. By the time he was eight, Norbert had read everything in reach and started wearing spectacles.

Specialist Wiener, engaged in trajectory research.

172   173

172 The Wiener family moved to Harvard, Massachusetts, and at the age of nine Norbert entered Ayer High School. At eleven, he graduated and entered Tufts College, where he graduated at fourteen. He received the Ph.D. from Harvard at eighteen and after service in a ballistic mathematics group during World War I became an instructor at M.I.T. in 1919.

173 Norbert Wiener was not only M.I.T.'s greatest genius but also its greatest campus character — the epitome of eccentricity and subject of many legends. ("Which way was I going when I met you?" he asked a colleague with whom he was chatting. The other professor told him. "Then I must have had lunch," said Wiener.) This cartoon by Chick Kane recalls his penchant for peanuts and ballistics. When Wiener talked in class about a ballistic trajectory around the moon, the students thought he was being ridiculously fanciful.

174 Wiener's *Nonlinear Problems in Random Theory* was put together from photographs (of which this is one) and tapes of his lectures by Yuk Wing Lee '27 and Amar G. Bose '51, of Electrical Engineering.

174

175

176

175   Claude E. Shannon, Donner Professor of Science and Professor of Electrical Engineering and Mathematics, worked as a Western Union messenger while in high school in Michigan and some fifteen years later laid the mathematical foundation for the modern telephone system's complexities. His *Mathematical Theory of Communication,* published by the Bell System in 1947–1948, is said to have provided the "thermodynamics of communication."

176   Isadore Singer, who is Norbert Wiener Professor of Mathematics, has made fundamental contributions to differential geometry, function algebras, partial differential equations, and operator algebras.

with head tilted back in an effort to overcome nearsightedness, he was usually puffing at the butt of a cigar and either laughing with a grunting chuckle at erudite jokes or moaning over the imminent doom of civilization. He could converse in thirteen languages, was a Sherlock Holmes fan, wrote science fiction, and published a number of books, including a novel.

While watching waves on the Charles River, Wiener conceived a new approach to a mathematical understanding of irregularities, and much of his work stemmed from his interest in describing and predicting random movements, as in molecules or electrical signals. His studies during World War II for antiaircraft predictors led to the publication of the "Yellow Peril," a book bound in yellow titled *Extrapolation, Interpolation and Smoothing of Stationary Times Series (with Engineering Applications).* The book had many uses.

Wiener is most popularly known as the founder of cybernetics, a term he derived from the Greek word "kubernetes," for steersman. This field represented his approach to an understanding of the methods by which a machine, an organism, or perhaps a social organization controls itself, particularly through the application of feedback. *The Human Use of Human Beings* was Wiener's popularized treatment of the subject.

Although M.I.T. was the home of cybernetics, the term is little used there because it is regarded as imprecise, having been employed so loosely throughout the world. The Russians once totally disapproved of Wiener, and *Pravda* denounced him as "a cigar-smoking tool of American capitalism," but there was a change in attitude and an Institute of Cybernetics was established. Wiener was invited to Russia for a cybernetics conference and hailed as a hero — the founding father.

Undoubtedly Wiener, who died in 1964, is the most universally remembered M.I.T. professor of the last fifty years. He was the most widely known throughout the world. His work continues to have an impact on many fields and it may be that posterity will regard him as the first great American mathematician.

In his day at M.I.T., at any rate, there was no one like him.

29

Into the Second Century

An alumnus recalls that his physics professor, Julius Stratton, once arrived at the classroom and announced, "There will be no class today. I apologize. I have not prepared."

There are innumerable ways for a professor to cover up in such a situation — such as giving a quiz. It is characteristic of Stratton that he would not bluff, and this may have been the only occasion in his life that he was not prepared. Earnest and thoughtful, warm yet dignified, impatient only with bad intentions or sloppy work, Stratton was well qualified as the president who would guide M.I.T. into its second century. "Jay and Kay" Stratton were popular among faculty, students, and alumni in the same way as "Jim and Liz" Killian.

Plans for the centennial celebration were in the making for a long time. It was agreed that when Killian returned from Washington it would be as chairman of the Corporation. Stratton, then "acting," would become president. Vannevar Bush, the chairman since 1957, would become honorary chairman. The changes were effective on January 1, 1959.

Because the centennial would be a time of academic festival, the inauguration of Stratton as president was a simple ceremony in Kresge Auditorium on Alumni Day, a time when old friends would be together. There was no long procession of delegates from other universities but greetings were brought from Harvard and Caltech, from the University of Washington which he had attended, and from the Swiss Federal Institute of Technology, where he earned his doctorate. His good friend William P. Allis said: "Julius, I bring you greetings from the Class of '23. We always knew you had it in you."

Observance of the centennial had two principal aspects, not unrelated. One was a series of events culminating in a week-long celebration in April of 1961. The other was the Second Century Fund campaign, launched in the spring of 1960 and continuing for three years. The goal, $66,000,000, would provide new buildings, endowed chairs, and funding for research. Killian had primary responsibility for the campaign.

177

177   In 1932 Julius Stratton and his colleague in physics William Allis crossed the Andes and traveled down the Amazon. Stratton is shown with Jivaro friends.

178   With a model showing the new buildings (in white) that they hoped to raise money for in the Second Century campaign are, left to right, President Stratton; John J. Wilson '29, chairman of the campaign; Alfred P. Sloan Jr. '95, honorary chairman; and Corporation Chairman Killian.

178

179

179   President Julius A. Stratton presided at the Centennial Assembly at which Prime Minister Harold Macmillan of Great Britain (center) was the speaker. At the prime minister's left are Sir Harold Anthony Caccia, British ambassador, and Dean John E. Burchard, Centennial chairman. At the extreme left is James McCormack '37, then vice-president of M.I.T.

One of the most important features of the Second Century program was the development of interdisciplinary centers, an organizational innovation that had been impressively successful in the case of the Research Laboratory of Electronics, formed under Stratton's direction.

The first of the new centers to be funded was the Center for Earth Sciences, which would bring together research in geology, geochemistry, geophysics, meteorology, and oceanography. Before the Second Century program was even announced, Dr. and Mrs. Cecil H. Green of Dallas, Texas, made a $6,000,000 contribution to it. Cecil Green was one of Stratton's 1923 classmates. Another member of the class, Uncas A. Whitaker of Harrisburg, Pennsylvania, and his wife Helen gave $2,100,000 (anonymously at the time) for the Center for the Life Sciences, providing quarters for biology, nutrition, and food science.

Although it was not initially in the Second Century program, a Center for Advanced Engineering Study was conceived by Alfred P. Sloan Jr., who was honorary chairman for the campaign, and the Sloan Foundation provided $5,000,000 for it. There were enough contributions to pay for a long-needed student center and other buildings. At the end of three years the campaign closed with an astounding total of $98,000,000.

The centennial celebration was a glittering event set in the middle of the Second Century campaign. As at the Mid-Century Convocation, its general chairman was John E. Burchard, a master at stage-managing big ideas and important personages. Prime Minister Harold Macmillan of Great Britain spoke and there were such prominent participants as Secretary of State Dean Rusk, J. Robert Oppenheimer, Sir John Cockroft, and Aldous Huxley (who had been a visiting professor at M.I.T. that year). The celebration reached a climax at an academic assembly (at which a newly designed fifteenth-century

180

180   The Student Center — Stratton Building — was designed by Eduardo Catalano, professor of architecture, with special attention to the need of students for a place to congregate — and even perhaps to loaf.

181   When the Class of 1916, which helped bring M.I.T. across the Charles River in the Bucentaur, held its fiftieth reunion, its leaders arrived in a replica (roughly speaking) of the famous barge to present a record gift of $3,100,000 to President Stratton. Joseph W. Barker is in the bow.

Venetian-style hat made its appearance on M.I.T. marshals) with an address by President Stratton.

Looking toward the second century, Stratton took note of the problems induced by science and technology, such as misuse of nuclear power, but said: "We have in our hands even now an almost limitless capacity to alter at will the material conditions of our existence. One can hardly conceive of a technological goal that will not yield to the engineer, if men will but put their minds and wills to the task. . . ."

Two years later, as the centennial receded into the past, President Stratton reviewed the Institute's growth and accomplishments and commented: "We must never forget that the unique product of a university — the basic reason for its being — is the student." He was not merely paying lip service to an ideal. Under his leadership there was extensive attention to revising the curriculum and teaching methods. A study was made, for example, by a Committee on Curriculum Content Planning, with Jerrold R. Zacharias as chairman, which resulted in greater flexibility and independence for students in their first two years.

Stratton participated in personal and lengthy consultation with undergraduates in the planning of a new women's residence and the student center. When the latter was completed in 1965, it was named, at the students' request, the Julius Adams Stratton Building.

The next year, reaching M.I.T.'s retirement age, Stratton went to New York as chairman of the Ford Foundation, a position of great responsibility since it involved developing new policies and finding a new president for the foundation — McGeorge Bundy. But after five years, he retired again, returned to M.I.T., and in a book-filled office, devoted his time to a study of its educational evolution.

181

In the same year that M.I.T. celebrated its centennial, Lincoln Laboratory celebrated its decennial with a memorable series of lectures. President Stratton doubtless had Lincoln in mind when he said in his centennial address, "One can hardly conceive of a technological goal that will not yield to the engineer." In a decade, Lincoln had demonstrated what high technology could accomplish, given goals and adequate funds.

The first goal was set following the Soviet Union's atomic overture of 1949, when it was clear that America was vulnerable to high-speed bombers streaking across the Arctic. The U.S. Air Force formed ADSEC — the Air Defense Systems Engineering Committee — to devise a means of protection. The chairman was George E. Valley Jr., a former Radiation Laboratory radar expert who, as a physics professor, was studying cosmic rays. The seven members included H. Guyford Stever, a young aeronautics professor who had been working on a missile project, and Charles S. Draper, for whom inertial guidance was more than a gleam in the eye. The newly formed Air Force Cambridge Research Laboratory, then a neighbor of M.I.T., was represented.

ADSEC saw the need for a system with greatly improved radars to spot enemy airplanes, high-speed computers to determine instantly where effective interception could be offered, and means for immediate dispatch of weapons — fighter planes or missiles.

M.I.T. had superior talent in radar and communications and it also had Whirlwind, not fully perfected and about to be abandoned for lack of funds. Valley and his committee arranged a test, linking radar with Whirlwind by telephone line to direct a fighter to intercept an approaching DC-3. The test was impressive and the Air Force asked M.I.T. to establish a laboratory to develop a system based on this method. President Killian expressed doubt that the Institute should take on so large a task. The Air Force insisted.

In Project Charles, a careful study was made of the program to be undertaken. By the middle of 1951, Project Lincoln was a going concern and the Air Force agreed to erect a new building for it at the M.I.T. Field Station (acquired for cosmic ray studies) adjoining Hanscom Field, in Lexington near the Lincoln town line. Researchers, who had been quartered in the old Radiation Laboratory buildings on the campus, began to move to the new Lincoln Laboratory in 1952.

Meanwhile the Research Laboratory of Electronics had been working on some of the problems that Lincoln faced. Jerome Wiesner, conducting research at Round Hill on broadcasting methods for the Voice of America (the Project Troy problem), developed a new idea for microwave communications: tropospheric scatter.

Microwaves were preferred for transmitting data. Unfortunately, microwave transmission was limited to line-of-sight, about thirty miles. But Wiesner and William Radford discovered that a powerful microwave beam could be bounced off the troposphere and transmitted a great distance. This over-the-horizon method would solve a serious problem in continental

30

High Technology at Lincoln Lab

182

182   Lincoln Laboratory in Lexington is a federal Contract Research Center operated by M.I.T. with its principal support from the Air Force, Army, Navy, and various other federal agencies. To its left in this view is L. G. Hanscom Field and to the right is Route 128, lined with industries, many of which have grown out of Lincoln and M.I.T. technological research.

183   In the complex developed by Lincoln Laboratory in Westford and Tyngsboro, Massachusetts, the Haystack Observatory is seen at a distance, the Millstone Hill Radar at the right, the Ionospheric Research Facility in the center, and a building housing a telescope for infrared radar research at the lower left.

183

defense. For early detection of an enemy there had to be radar installations in the far north. The problem was how to get information to command headquarters without establishing a large number of microwave relay stations — difficult and costly in a frozen wilderness. Tropospheric scatter transmission would provide the data links. Out of a summer study at Lincoln Laboratory in 1952 came plans for the DEW Line — Distant Early Warning Line. Surveillance radars would be strung across the top of the continent, from Alaska to Greenland.

Jay W. Forrester assumed direction of Lincoln's Digital Computer Division and set about improving Whirlwind, which was linked to radar at Truro in the Cape Cod System for experimental work. To keep track of all enemy and defense craft, a huge computer memory was needed and the new magnetic cores took care of that. Later even better computers were built, including the first transistorized one.

With this kind of progress, the SAGE System was developed. SAGE stood for Semi-Automatic Ground Environment. It was automatic in that data on the status of an air battle (or battles, in case of simultaneous attacks from different directions) would be processed by computers and presented visually on scopes. It was "Semi-" in that the military command would make decisions about dispatching interceptor planes or defensive missiles.

By 1953 the possibility of intercontinental ballistic missiles was real. Out of studies at Lincoln came plans for BMEWS (pronounced Be-muse) — the Ballistic Missile Early Warning System — which required enormous radars in the North for detecting and tracking.

By 1958 the first sector of the SAGE System was operational and the project was entering a phase involving contracts for large-scale construction and manufacturing. M.I.T. believed this was beyond the limits of innovative research appropriate for a university and organized an independent, non-profit agency, the Mitre Corporation, to assume such responsibilities. Some five hundred people engaged in the SAGE work were transferred from Lincoln to Mitre.

This was a pivotal year for Lincoln. Since it had accomplished what it first set out to do, the question arose whether it should continue to operate. The Air Force pledged long-term support and President Stratton agreed to continue within "our areas of technical competence and recognizing our responsibilities as an educational institution." There was increasing interchange between Lincoln and the campus.

For research toward an Anti-Intercontinental Ballistic Missile system, Lincoln built a huge 84-foot steerable radar at Millstone Hill, forty miles northwest of Cambridge. This radar came into operation just before the first Sputnik was launched and immediately proved its value by tracking the Russian satellite. Later at Millstone Hill, Lincoln erected a 220-foot, zenith-pointing reflector for ionospheric research and the 120-foot Haystack dish, not only huge but extremely precise. More recently it has installed a four-foot telescope for laser radar, using infrared for long-range probing.

184 The SCR–radar developed in World War II by the Radiation Laboratory (on the trailer) could track an airplane at about 50 miles. The big dish built by Lincoln Laboratory at Wallops Island, Virginia, for reentry research could track a target the size of a baseball 100 miles away.

184

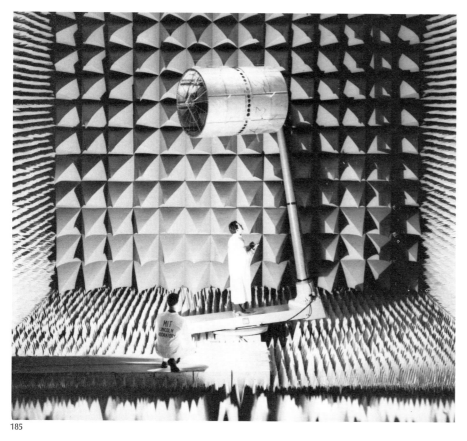

185

186

185   LES-6, one of a series of space communications satellites launched by Lincoln Laboratory, was tested in a microwave anechoic chamber before being sent on its experimental mission.

186   This is the first message sent through space by television. The signal was bounced off the Echo I balloon satellite by Lincoln Laboratory and received by its station in California.

Lincoln pioneered in communication by satellite. The first experiment was in Project West Ford, when the laboratory put copper dipoles into orbit, providing a reflecting band from which microwave signals could be bounced to a distant station. Unfortunately the dipoles, which were tiny, hairlike fibers, were first referred to as "needles" and the public was alarmed by the thought of their raining down from space (though actually they would burn up like meteorites). Some astronomers objected that they would clutter up the firmament, but their fears proved greatly exaggerated.

Active satellites, which could relay signals electronically, were more desirable anyhow when they were proved feasible, and the laboratory launched a series of Lincoln Experimental Satellites, starting with LES-1 in early 1965. Ten years later LES-8 and LES-9 were prepared for launching to demonstrate satellite-to-satellite communication in synchronous orbit.

Lincoln's activities have become more and more diverse. It has opened up new regions in the radio and optical spectrum, from Extremely Low Frequencies, about one hertz (one cycle per second), to one thousand million megahertz, in the ultraviolet. It has made significant contributions in radio and radar astronomy, worldwide seismic detection, high-field-strength superconducting magnets, air traffic control, ambulatory health care, and various laser applications, from spectroscopy to air pollution measurement.

31

Science Is Coeducational

Ellen Swallow broke through the male bulwark of M.I.T., but it was 1883 before women were admitted freely to all courses and 1960 before they were really welcomed. The number dropped to as low as 14 in 1915. Even in 1950, when total enrollment passed 5,000, only 76 students were women.

There were various reasons for the lag (which Women's Lib would ascribe to male chauvinism). Relatively few women were interested in engineering and science, few were adequately prepared in mathematics and physics, and they were not likely to be encouraged by parents and teachers. Career expectations were limited. And M.I.T., with a rough-and-ready, Tech-Is-Hell tradition, did not attract them. A common argument against their admission was that, having deprived eligible men of places at the Institute, they were likely to get married and "waste" their technical education.

A practical argument was that the Institute, hard-pressed to provide facilities for men, could not offer adequate living and recreational quarters for women. And M.I.T., as well as other colleges, believed that girls needed a special kind of sheltering.

An alumna, Mrs. Katharine Dexter McCormick, provided a solution to that problem. She was the great-granddaughter of Senator Samuel Dexter of Boston, who served as secretary of war under President John Adams. Her father, a prominent Chicago attorney, died when she was young, and she and her mother moved to Boston. She decided she wanted to go to M.I.T. and because she "grew up on French and music," she had to spend four years as a special student before she could pass the entrance examination and be admitted in 1900 as one of 44 women among 2,500 men.

187   Two dozen women students at M.I.T. in 1888. At the extreme left in the rear is Ellen Swallow Richards. Sixth from the left is Marion Talbot, who with her started the organization that became the AAUW. She was later a dean at the University of Chicago.

188

While at M.I.T., Katharine Dexter was courted by a Princeton man, Stanley McCormick, son of the wealthy Cyrus McCormick of reaper fame, and shortly after she received a degree in biology in 1904 they were married. Three years later he fell ill and she devoted much of her life to caring for him.

Mrs. McCormick found time, however, to be a leader in the women's suffrage movement and when, having won the vote, the National Woman Suffrage Association reorganized as the League of Women Voters, she was elected vice-president. She also was a foremost supporter of research in birth control.

Beginning in 1945, faculty wives, led by Mrs. Compton, sponsored a small residence for women in Back Bay and Mrs. McCormick helped by paying for taxis to take them to the Institute in inclement weather. In 1960 she decided to provide funds for a women's residence on the campus as a memorial to her husband. James Killian and Julius Stratton agreed that M.I.T. should actively encourage women to enter.

The first tower of McCormick Hall was completed in 1963 and Mrs. McCormick was so pleased that she provided funds for a second tower, which was finished a few months after her death in 1967. It turned out that she had left the bulk of her estate to M.I.T., bringing her total contributions to the astounding total of $32,700,000. In her will she explained: "Since my graduation in 1904 I have wished to express my gratitude to the Institute for its advanced policy of scientific training for women. This policy gave me the opportunity to obtain the scientific training which has been of inestimable value to me throughout my life."

188   Katharine Dexter in a biology laboratory, probably in the year she graduated, 1904. She later explained that she was wearing a hat because she had been to a social function and stopped in the lab to work on an experiment at the time a photographer showed up.

189   Mrs. Katharine McCormick (left) was undaunted by the rain when she marched with Mrs. H. Carpenter for women's suffrage in Chicago in 1917.

190   Mrs. McCormick made a rare public appearance — for her later years — at the dedication of the first tower of Stanley McCormick Hall in 1963. Others are Chairman James R. Killian Jr., President Julius A. Stratton, Mrs. Killian, Mrs. Stratton, Margaret MacVicar '64, president of the Undergraduate Women's Association, and Mrs. Karl T. Compton.

189

190

191 McCormick Hall, by providing living and recreation quarters for women, enabled M.I.T. to open the door.

192 Florence Luscomb, an architecture graduate of 1909, sold a suffragette paper at the edge of Boston Common for two years and went to Washington to march in a demand for the vote the day before President Wilson's inauguration.

193 Some sixty years later Florence Luscomb was still speaking out, this time at the big peace rally in Washington on April 24, 1971. She practiced architecture for a few years but devoted most of her career as a worker in various unpopular causes. At the age of eighty-eight she was still at it.

191

192

193

194

195 The first woman to be dean for student affairs, Dr. Carola B. Eisenberg, was appointed in 1972. In her leisure she does needlepoint and she discovered that at the same time she was working on a version of the M.I.T. seal, a student, Albert L. Oliver Jr., had undertaken the same project.

195 Karen Henry, then a sophomore, was chosen queen of the campus carnival in 1965 and was robed by Dean Frederick G. Fassett Jr. She went on to get a degree in naval architecture and marine engineering.

McCormick Hall provided rooms for 239 students, and this automatically increased the number of women who could be admitted. Furthermore, the rules were relaxed and required only freshmen (women and men) to live on the campus. Then several men's dormitories went coeducational. So did some fraternities. Housing for women was no longer a problem.

Meanwhile, of course, profound changes were occurring in the status of women everywhere. They were better prepared in high school for science and engineering and those fields beckoned to them. There was a revolution in mores, due in part to the Pill. Marriage and housewifery were no longer an almost inevitable choice of occupation. Women's Lib clamored and, even if not vocal, most young women took a new view of the equality of the sexes.

M.I.T. made a determined effort to attract more women. Their applications for the Class of 1978 were up 93 percent and 214 entered as freshmen. The female student population for 1974–1975 was 1,060 — plus 229 from Wellesley College in the exchange program. That was still a minority in a total student body of 7,749, but a potent minority.

The number of women on the faculty was being increased as rapidly as qualified candidates could be attracted. The dean for student affairs — by tradition an exemplar of robust masculine virtues — was a woman, Dr. Carola B. Eisenberg, and not an engineer but a psychiatrist.

When President Stratton dedicated the David Flett du Pont Athletic Center in 1959 he observed: "Society asks more of most men than sheer intellectual ability — it demands also moral hardiness, self-discipline, a competitive spirit, and other qualities that in more old-fashioned terms we might call character."

That explains — if any explanation is needed — why M.I.T. has built a program of athletics with emphasis on participation rather than on sending a football team to the Rose Bowl. It competes in 22 intercollegiate sports — more than any other college; but of greater significance is the fact that some 6,000 students take part in athletics, which may consist of playing on one of the 800 intramural teams or joining a cricket, white water, or karate club.

Writing in *Sports Illustrated* in 1975, John Underwood was impressed with such figures and indicated amazement that

M.I.T. equips and fields all these teams without offering or granting a single athletic scholarship; without recruiting a single athlete, be he blue, red or white chip; without charging a nickel of admission to any event; without caring, really, if anybody shows up to watch, which is always a possibility. . . .

Encouraged to leave their intellectual cocoons, given time and opportunity, the true scholar-athletes emerge at M.I.T. . . . Some of them actually get good.

Sailing demonstrates the philosophy of keen competition and wide participation. M.I.T. practically invented sailing as an intercollegiate sport and has won more championships than any other school. It had the first dinghy facility in the country, introducing the 12½-foot boat designed by George Owen '94, professor of naval architecture, in 1935. The Tech Dinghy set the standard for college racing, but M.I.T.'s fleet of some four dozen boats includes other classes.

Walter C. "Jack" Wood '17, who was sailing master for twenty-seven years, can be thanked for much of M.I.T.'s success. He was founder of the Intercollegiate Yacht Racing Association of North America Hall of Fame at Annapolis and he and eight other M.I.T. sailors were elected to membership. Four Tech men went to the Olympics and two have won the Prince of Wales Trophy in North American championships. Sailing was the first sport at M.I.T. to have a women's varsity team. And in addition to all of those students who participate in college racing, there are about a thousand members of the Institute community who sail on the Charles for pleasure.

The one sport in which M.I.T. competes on what are regarded as big-league terms is crew racing. Tech crews have performed well, and without special recruiting or athletic scholarships. When Jack H. Frailey '44, a crew coach, was appointed director of student financial aid, someone wise-cracked that M.I.T. was the only college at which a coach could be appointed to such a job without suspicion of motives.

32

Athletics for Character

196

197

198

196   Representatives of all 22 intercollegiate sports were assembled in 1975 and performed for M.I.T. photographer Calvin Campbell.

197   George J. Leness '26 won the New England Intercollegiate half-mile championship on the old East Campus track in his senior year. He became a member of the Corporation in 1949.

198   On the first varsity crew were, left to right, John C. Molinar '22, stroke; Horace W. McCurdy '22; Colby W. Bryden '22; Wilbur J. Woodruff '22; Irving D. Jakobson '21; Walter B. Driscoll '22; Donald G. Morse '21; and Clift R. Richards '22. The coxswain was T. O. M. Davidson '21.

199

200

199   Jubilant M.I.T. crewmen displayed captured Harvard shirts after they beat eleven shells in the Eastern sprint regatta at Annapolis in 1950. Two weeks earlier they had been defeated by Harvard by one foot.

200   The 1954 lightweights won their first national championship and were the first M.I.T. crew to go to Henley, where they won the Thames Challenge Cup. Left to right, they are Valdemar Skov '55, Robert F. Buntschuh '55, William H. McTigue '54, Robert N. Sawyer '56, Larry Holmes '54, Leonard V. Gallagher '54, and Robert D. Wilkes '55. Jack H. Frailey '44 was the coach and Jerome D. Waye '54, the coxswain.

The first M.I.T. crew was organized, as a club, in 1910, but after two years of promising competition, rowing went to an interclass status. A varsity crew was organized in 1920 and did so well in its first two seasons that M.I.T. bought the Boston Athletic Association boathouse and took the sport seriously. Tech won its first major regatta in 1924. Horace W. McCurdy '22, a member of the 1920 crew and one of the first captains, was a leader in raising funds for a new boathouse — among the best in the country — completed in 1966.

Through the years, with leaders such as John A. Rockwell '96, Allan W. Rowe '01, Ralph T. Jope '28, and a host of dedicated coaches, M.I.T. conducted a vigorous athletic program. It committed itself to comprehensive development in 1945 with the appointment of the first director of athletics, Ivan J. Geiger, a three-letter man from Ohio State who during the war had assisted Jack Dempsey in training Coast Guardsmen. "Ike" Geiger died at the age of forty-five in 1955. In an editorial, *The Tech* observed: "He was always happy when an M.I.T. team won, but he was prouder when some four hundred students used Briggs Field for soccer, football and tennis in a single afternoon."

201

202

201   This was the original Tech Dinghy, designed by Professor George Owen, which became a standard in college sailing.

202   Sailing was the first sport to have a women's varsity team. This is Mary Anne Bradford, who won a singles championship in 1973.

203

203   Deborah Stein '76 was the first woman to win a place on a varsity team to compete with men, qualifying in cross-country skiing.

204   Tennis got a big lift when the J. B. Carr Indoor Tennis Center was installed in 1971. Jasper B. Carr '16, who gave the inflated dome and courts, played in an exhibition match at the dedication with Vic Seixas as his partner.

Richard L. Balch, who came from Stanford, and Ross H. Smith, who succeeded him in 1961, extended the program of competitiveness and maximum participation, at the same time fostering close personal relationships with students. "Jim" Smith, who was All-America in soccer, All–New England in lacrosse, and who won his letter in basketball at Springfield College, came from coaching at Cornell. He has been a leader nationally in athletic organizations.

Under Smith's direction, opportunities for women in athletics have increased and now in nine of the twenty-two intercollegiate sports women have varsity teams. This has intensified the use of the Du Pont Center, the Armory and Rockwell Cage, and a new building, which among other things will accommodate indoor hockey and track, is being planned. Erection of the "pneumatic" J. B. Carr Indoor Tennis Center, named for Jasper B. Carr '16, in 1971, made possible year-round tennis, a sport of growing popularity.

204

The dedication of the Center for Materials Science and Engineering in 1965 was an important milestone in the history of a field that was founded one hundred years before as "Geology and Mining." The Department of Metallurgy, split off from moribund Mining, was established in 1937 and, under President Compton's leadership, a scientific approach was undertaken by a branch of engineering that had been dominated by the empirical.

In the prewar years, the metallurgy faculty acquired such people as John Chipman, a physical chemist, and John Wulff, a physicist. During the war those two worked on uranium and various members of the faculty were diverted to other military problems. Frederick H. Norton '18 directed a center at M.I.T. for Manhattan Project to develop wholly new kinds of ceramics for crucibles to be used in making the bomb. His brother, John T. Norton '18, worked on armor plate. (A third brother, Charles L. Norton Jr. '25, had also once been a member of the department. Their father, Charles Norton Sr. '93, was a physics professor for forty-six years.)

It was not until after the war that the department really gained momentum in its new scientific approach. Chipman made distinguished contributions to improvements in steelmaking through his research involving very fine measurements on the effects of hydrogen, oxygen, and other elements. Morris

33

Metal Is a Material

205   Casting metal in the old foundry was a dramatic activity that required steady nerves and strong muscles. This picture was made about 1952. The foundry was closed in 1967.

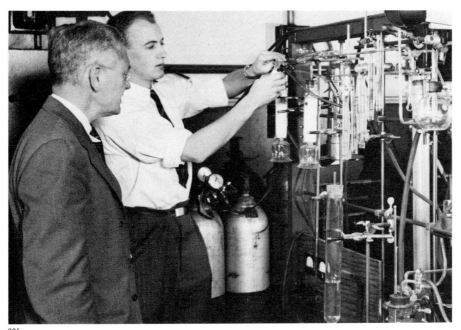

206

206   John Chipman (left), who joined the Department of Metallurgy in 1937, brought to it a chemist's competence in analyzing metallurgical processes and he made important advances, especially in steelmaking. He is shown with David B. Smith '52, then a graduate student.

207   Merton C. Flemings Jr. '51 has been experimenting with methods by which molten metal is stirred into a mushy form like soft ice cream before it is cast. It enters the mold like toothpaste. The method achieves desirable characteristics in the metal when it solidifies and is expected to make possible greater automation in foundry methods.

Cohen '33 was another leader in developing an understanding of the atomic and molecular structure of metals and in the teaching of this new kind of metallurgy. Fred Norton's work in ceramics led into new, nonmetallic areas, such as the study of ice as a structural material by W. David Kingery '48. (The Air Force was interested in the use of ice, reinforced with fiberglass, for constructing airfields and buildings in the Arctic.) The rise of semiconductors focused attention on crystalline forms of new materials.

It was with this background that Chipman, Cohen, and Nicholas J. Grant '44 began talking about a new strategy in materials research and suggested to representatives of the Advanced Research Projects Agency of the Department of Defense that it support interdisciplinary projects. Ironically, in adopting the idea, ARPA decided M.I.T. was already so competent in the field that it would have to give first support to other universities. Finally, however, it did make a grant to M.I.T. that permitted construction of the Center for Materials Science and Engineering.

Meanwhile, professors from other departments, notably John Slater of physics and Peter Elias of electrical engineering, had joined the metallurgists in the development of research in materials. Arthur R. von Hippel, director of the Laboratory for Insulation Research, had demonstrated the usefulness of molecular engineering.

Professors and students from seven departments now work together in the center. Grant is the director and the largest number are what had once been called "metallurgists." But in 1975, at the request of the new department head, Walter S. Owen, the name, which had evolved to Department of Metallurgy and Materials Science, was changed to Materials Science and Engineering.

207

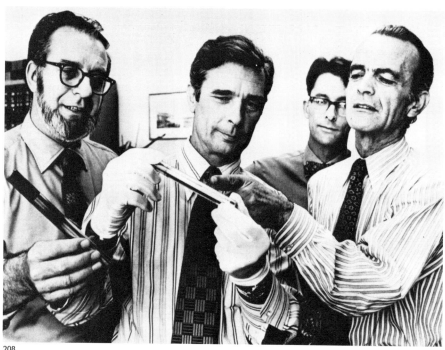

208

209

208   Zero-gravity growing of crystals was a highly successful experiment on Skylab in 1973 arranged by the Center for Materials Science and Engineering. The experiment was conducted by two professors, Harry G. Gatos '50 (right) and August F. Witt (center), who holds a quartz ampule containing the first crystals. At left is Clifford Herman, an engineering assistant, and in the rear, Manfred Lichtensteiger of the center's research staff.

209   Howard W. Johnson, chairman of the M.I.T. Corporation, presented a section of a Skylab crystal to President Gerald Ford. At left is James C. Fletcher, administrator of the National Aeronautics and Space Administration.

210   The diversity of materials that are studied in the Center for Materials Science and Engineering is indicated by the research in which two postdoctoral biophysicists are engaged — a study of the lens of the eye. Toyoichi Tanaka (left) and Dave Nicoli direct an argon laser beam through a lens to measure the scattering of light by protein clumps that cause cataracts. Experiments with rabbits show that early detection of cataracts is possible. Nonsurgical treatment may be developed.

210

"Industrial management has passed through a long process of development as our industrial age has evolved," Alfred P. Sloan Jr. once said. "Today it has become in every sense of the word a matter of science."

Most scientists would deny that management is a science — and so would most managers. But it was through a rational approach to corporate operations that Alfred Sloan put General Motors together a half-century ago, and the school that bears his name applies the rigorous analytical methods of science in seeking to understand economic tides and the human complexities of the marketplace. The Alfred P. Sloan School of Management could appropriately have been named for him even if he had not been its chief benefactor.

The concept of rational analysis in the education of future managers was established long before the Sloan School was founded and even before Alfred Sloan, a quiet, methodical electrical engineering student, graduated from M.I.T. in 1895. This is one thing that President Francis A. Walker had in mind when he introduced solid economics studies and recruited Davis R. Dewey, who became a leading teacher in the field.

In 1914, Dewey organized Course XV, in engineering administration, a course which has produced many of the Institute's most eminent alumni. When Erwin H. Schell became head of the new Department of Business and Engineering Administration in 1930 he was eager not only to develop the undergraduate program further but also to attract graduate students. He carried through the idea of offering fellowships to engineering graduates of "unusual promise." Alfred Sloan and five other members of the Corporation each put up $1,500 for the fellowships and a few years later Sloan began to provide the principal support. In 1938, the original plan became the Sloan Fellowship program, in which young executives were sponsored by companies and other organizations for a full year of study. There have been, so far, 1,112 Sloan Fellows from all over the world.

At his fiftieth reunion in 1945, Sloan endowed a professorship in management and began thinking of helping to create a school. The idea took shape when toward the end of 1950 the Sloan Foundation made a grant of $5,250,000 to found the School of Industrial Management. About half the grant was used to buy the building at 50 Memorial Drive that Lever Brothers Company was abandoning to move its headquarters to New York.

Edward Pennell Brooks '17, who happened to have been the first graduate of Course XV, was appointed the first dean of the new school in 1952. Having been with Sears, Roebuck & Co. for twenty-four years, he combined managerial skill with a zest for intellectual enterprise. The school moved into what was now known as the Sloan Building, along with the Department of Economics and Social Science, a happy symbiosis since they could provide complementary academic strength. And there was room for the Dewey Library, named for the grand old man of economics, which they could share. Pressures of expansion were relieved a dozen years later when the Grover M. Hermann Building was built next door, providing space for the library

34

Science in Management

211

212

211   Among the great names associated
with M.I.T. — those of presidents, scientists,
engineers, and other leaders — the name
of Alfred P. Sloan Jr. will always be remembered. When he died in 1966 at the age of
ninety, he had been a member of the Corporation for forty years — a devoted alumnus,
friendly critic, wise counselor, and generous
patron. The exact extent of his generosity
is difficult to determine, for one should include grants made by the Alfred P. Sloan
Foundation, which, although under the management of an independent board, was not
likely to ignore the wishes of the founder. All
together, his gifts and the foundation grants
over a period of 56 years totaled $64,620,358
— by far the largest amount attributable to
a private source.

Mr. Sloan (though he had warmth and hu-
mor he was inclined to be formal, and first
names were never used in exchanges with Institute friends) took a special interest in the
Sloan School of Management, the Sloan Building that it occupies, the Sloan Fellows, and
the Sloan Professorship of Management. His
interests are also reflected by the names of the
Sloan Metals Processing Laboratory, the Sloan
Automotive Laboratories, and other Sloan
professorships. Although the Center for Advanced Engineering Study does not bear
his name, he conceived the idea for its establishment and the foundation provided the
funds. This picture was made in 1963 when
plans for the center were announced.

212   Dean Howard W. Johnson (left) succeeded Edward Pennell "Penn" Brooks
'17, who was the first management graduate
and the first dean of the Sloan School.

213

and other facilities. It was at this time that the name of the school was changed to Alfred P. Sloan School of Management.

Dropping "Industrial" from the name was no accident, for the scope of the school's interests was steadily widening, including such areas as health care systems and public policy. Two of the great teachers were Douglass V. Brown and Douglas M. McGregor, the one in labor and the other in organization. And class after class was excited by the humanist's perspective offered by historian Elting E. Morison.

A school never bound by tradition was receptive when Jay W. Forrester, electrical engineer, decided to switch his career to management in 1956. Having developed Whirlwind and led in the planning of the SAGE System at Lincoln Laboratory, he conceived of a way to apply computer techniques and feedback principles to business in what he called industrial dynamics. Hundreds of variables could be simulated to determine the probable consequences of strategic or tactical decisions, and such analysis often produced startling implications.

Having jolted industrial dogma, Forrester proceeded to apply his method to urban dynamics, working with John F. Collins, the former mayor of Boston who had become consulting professor of urban affairs. They came to the

213   Elting E. Morison (with feet on desk), an industrial historian, enriched the educational experiences of Sloan Fellows for years. He was captured by the Yale faculty but later returned as the first Elizabeth and James Killian 1926 Professor, accredited at large to the School of Humanities and Social Science.

214

215

214   Daniel Quinn Mills, who teaches labor management, in a postclass session with James H. Williams, Ashok Khanna, and S. Tharuvai Ananthhnarayanan, graduate students.

215   The editors of the *Sloan Management Review* in 1975 were Michael B. Green, Sandra Fiebelkorn, and Margery R. Weil, all graduate students.

conclusion that some policies intended to improve urban life may have just the opposite effect.

World problems were the next targets for systems analysis. Using the Forrester method, a group based at M.I.T. projected population growth, food supply, industrial output, and other variables to the year 2100 and in a study titled "The Limits to Growth" came up with a frightening picture of Malthusian disaster. The conclusions were not universally accepted.

The school's interests had begun to be international a number of years before, an example being the organization of summer programs for executives in India by Howard W. Johnson in 1960. Johnson, who had been director of management programs at the University of Chicago Industrial Relations Center, joined the school in 1955 as director of the Sloan Fellowship Program. At the age of thirty-three, he was as young as many Sloans and, with a nimble, challenging mind, was ideally suited to lead them in intellectual adventuring. The next year he organized a program for senior executives that proved successful, and when Penn Brooks retired in 1959 succeeded him as dean.

William F. Pounds succeeded Howard Johnson as dean in 1966. With degrees in chemical engineering and mathematical economics from Carnegie Tech and experience at Eastman Kodak, he had joined the faculty in 1961, taught in the program in India, and organized a management program in Colombia. He extended activities into such fields as urban affairs and health care management.

In a review at the end of the Sloan School's first twenty years, Dean Pounds pointed out that its original assumption was that research could contribute new concepts to management, "an important departure from the strategy underlying schools of business and management up to that time." He commented: "It is now clear that the early decision to proceed along these lines was sound, and now the strategy which has guided the Sloan School for the past 20 years is rapidly being undertaken by other schools around the world."

216   Paul W. MacAvoy, who is Henry R. Luce Professor of Environment and Public Policy in the Sloan School of Management, was appointed by President Ford to the Council of Economic Advisors in 1975. His research has been particularly concerned with the relationships of government and industry in such areas as energy, transportation, and communications.

216

As dean of the Sloan School of Management, Howard W. Johnson had a special interest in executive development programs. In 1965 it became evident that his own managerial skill was recognized. He was offered, and he accepted, a position as executive vice-president of a major American company.

Meanwhile, the M.I.T. Corporation Committee on Succession had been considering the choice of a new president, to succeed Julius Stratton when he retired the next year. In December, the committee chose Johnson. With a loyalty to the Institute, a commitment to education, and a readiness to accept a challenge, he accepted, relinquishing the other position.

On the day after he took office, July 1, 1966, Johnson turned forty-four, the same age as James R. Killian was when he became president. Killian and Francis Amasa Walker had proved that a great president of M.I.T. need not be a scientist, but if any members of the faculty were apprehensive because of Johnson's lack of background in science and engineering they were reassured when he selected as provost the dean of science, Jerome B. Wiesner. And, while Johnson was hardly a novice on the national scene, he had abundant backup from two former science advisers to the President of the United States, Wiesner and Killian, the latter continuing to devote full time to the Institute as chairman of the Corporation.

In his inaugural address on October 7, President Johnson referred to M.I.T. as "a university that never looks back as a conserver of the past but always forward as a maker of the future." He recognized his responsibility as a manager of change. He said:

I believe that the general range of problems attacked by M.I.T. in the future will shift more and more to those that understandably affect the ways in which our society lives, that this institution will increasingly exert its power toward problems of human significance. It seems clear to me that we have reached the stage of population levels and aspirations when the happy and productive ordering of our community lies in massive solutions to our problems in education, urban living, in regional development, in commerce and industry, in transportation, in medicine, and, yes, in the peaceful conduct of nations. And the effective solutions to these problems become of first priority in the nation.

In the area of medicine, there was major accomplishment when President Johnson and President Nathan Pusey of Harvard reached an agreement through which the joint Harvard-M.I.T. Program in Health Sciences and Technology was developed. A large variety of educational and research activities in collaboration with Harvard Medical School was thereby made possible.

In an attack on urban problems, almost every M.I.T. department became engaged in the search, frequently through interdisciplinary effort, for solutions — in transportation, housing, race relations, municipal services.

35

Managing Change

217

A number of the new endeavors, as well as such activities as the interdisciplinary laboratories, became the responsibilities of Provost Wiesner. To aid him and to give special attention to educational experiments and curriculum development, Paul E. Gray '54 was appointed assistant and then associate provost. As time went on, the latter devoted intensive effort to a long-range program of equal opportunity for minorities, especially blacks — to recruiting them as students and to seeking to overcome their disadvantages, and to increasing their numbers on faculty and staff. Walter A. Rosenblith, after serving for two years as chairman of the faculty, was also appointed associate provost and concentrated his skills on the intricacies of developing programs in health sciences and urban affairs. For a year he was acting director of the Joint Center for Urban Studies.

As chairman of the Corporation, Killian had the responsibility for community affairs and for searching for funds — a crucial task because of inflation and the instability of federal support. And the need of a private institution for private funds is never-ending. In its concern for the community, M.I.T. initiated a remarkable and unprecedented program of housing for the elderly in Cambridge.

The Institute was at the same time trying to fulfill its own building needs. The Camille Dreyfus Building for Chemistry and a building for computer services were completed and funds were being sought for an electrical

217   Chairman James R. Killian Jr. extends a congratulating hand after presenting the M.I.T. charter to Howard W. Johnson at his inauguration as president. At right is Vannevar Bush, honorary chairman of the Corporation.

218

218   At a press conference in 1967 an announcement was made that the Ford Foundation had granted $3,000,000 apiece to Harvard and M.I.T. for urban studies. From the left, President Nathan Pusey of Harvard; Daniel P. Moynihan, director of the Joint Center for Urban Studies; President Howard W. Johnson; Thomas D. Cabot, chairman of the M.I.T. Corporation Visiting Committee for the Department of City and Regional Planning; and Lloyd Rodwin, chairman of the faculty committee for the Joint Center.

engineering building. Housing for students had high priority. Eastgate for married students was built and a new high-rise building at Westgate for single graduate students was started. Burton-Conner House was completely renovated and MacGregor House, the first new men's dormitory in two decades, was added. A second half of McCormick Hall was completed in 1968, permitting a substantial increase in the number of women admitted to M.I.T. Howard Johnson strongly favored policies that would provide equal opportunities for women. And in 1967 he and President Ruth M. Adams of Wellesley College developed a plan permitting cross-registration of M.I.T. and Wellesley students. This program brought more women to the campus in Cambridge and made available to M.I.T. the excellent and different educational resources of Wellesley.

While presiding over a complex and rapidly changing university, Johnson contended with mounting student-impelled distractions such as no other M.I.T. president had ever experienced. The war in Vietnam was, of course, the focus for unrest, and aside from the view that it was a bad war (with which almost everyone at M.I.T. agreed), it had a personal and tragic meaning for youth.

But the revulsion for war was only one aspect of a cultural revolution that was taking place to the tune of mind-blowing rock music reverberating from the Mersey's shore — a revolution against adult authority, educational conformity, sexual convention, suburban morality, middle-class aspirations, and political hypocrisy, to name a few targets. Liberation of hair and costume was the symbol. Charcoal gray uniforms disappeared and the self-dramatizing look of the student population became that of a wild masquerade. In any crowd one could spot Raskolnikov, John the Baptist, Karl Marx, Fu Manchu, Ché Guevara, Madame Defarge, and a host of other characters including ploughboys (barefooted) from the Bronx and booted insurrectionists from Winnetka. Their convictions and methods were almost as varied as their costumes.

For a long time M.I.T. had seemed immune to the violent protests that shook Columbia, Berkeley, and other universities. "The wave of demonstrations against the Dow Chemical Company which had swept U.S. college campuses this year gently lapped against M.I.T.'s shores in November," reported *Technology Review* after a sit-in at the Placement Office in 1967. As time went on, the waves grew higher. Through some four years there were sit-ins, teach-ins, sleep-ins, demonstrations, confrontations, occupations, and denunciations, the latter in millions of words — ugly ones — screamed, printed, paraded, and scrawled on walls.

Just before the first Dow protest, President Johnson had issued a statement that said, in part: "It is a principle of the university to permit, provide, and protect an environment where dissent is possible. I hope that visitors to our campus will understand this. On the other hand, it is important that such protest not become violent or abusive or interfere or limit the reasonable rights of others in the process."

The word "reasonable" was at the heart of the whole M.I.T. philosophy. Administrators were willing to engage in reasonable discussion of any subject. Unreason, however, was a tactical weapon of the protestors. Hoping to "radicalize" the entire student body and faculty, using inflammatory language, making wild charges in revolutionary jargon, the leaders sought to demonstrate that the Institute was a malignant, ruthless arm of a military dictatorship. In response, Howard Johnson refused to regard the students as enemies. He struggled to keep lines of communications open, to cooperate in rational solutions to real problems, and, above all, to prevent an irreparable split in the faculty. He succeeded, and the faculty did hold together, probably more effectively than at any other major university in the country. For example, there was a solid vote to retain ROTC, almost unique in the Northeast.

In the main, despite interruptions, M.I.T. went about its business. The policy of being reasonable prevailed. Perhaps most students found that revolutionary doctrine offered no substitutes for intellectual integrity, respect for human rights, a belief in the "improvability" of man, and the capacity for change that have made M.I.T. a great institution.

219

221

"MAN, THAT'S REALLY TELLING IT LIKE IT IS....!"

222

219   On Alumni Day in 1969, SACC, the Science Action Coordinating Committee, made up chiefly of graduate students, rallied at the Student Center and sought to intrude on a panel discussion of "The Human Purpose." As was usually the case at such rallies, the crowd was salted with a good many administrators, as observers prepared to take any action that seemed appropriate. At the left of the large placard are Dean for Student Affairs Kenneth R. Wadleigh and Assistant Provost Paul E. Gray, and at the extreme left and lower, Walter A. Rosenblith, chairman of the faculty.

220   In November of 1969, protesters set up a picket line to prevent staff members from entering the Instrumentation Laboratory, at the left, where work was done on Polaris and Poseidon guidance systems. Cambridge sent police to enforce the law against obstructive picketing on a public way. The protesters were routed.

221   Throughout the period of protests, faculty meetings were frequent and long, serving as an indispensable means of communication and clarification and providing an opportunity for professors to participate in shaping policy. Howard Johnson presided with patience and fairness, giving an example of a cool and reasonable approach to problems. The speaker in this picture at Kresge Auditorium is Jeffrey I. Steinfeld '62, of chemistry.

222   This is the way cartoonist Paul Conrad of the *Los Angeles Times* visualized protests at M.I.T. in 1969.

223

223   Students who took a negative and violent approach to national problems were in the minority. An example of those with a constructive approach were the participants in the Clean Air Car Race to demonstrate that technology could deal with pollution. With various kinds of innovative power, 43 cars representing colleges started from M.I.T. for the race to California in August of 1970. M.I.T. entries are in the center foreground, an electric hybrid and a turbine. The race grew out of the Great Electric Car Race in 1968 between M.I.T. and California Institute of Technology.

Changes did occur, though not necessarily as a result of protests. A fundamental one was an increase in informality and flexibility in relationships within the Institute. Representation in governance became broader. Educational reform had been in progress for years and in many respects it was accelerated, partly through the work of a major Commission on Education appointed by Johnson. Questions long had been raised about the appropriateness of some research at the Instrumentation Laboratory as part of an educational institution. After extensive studies, begun by a panel headed by Dean William F. Pounds, a process to divest the laboratory (renamed the Charles Stark Draper Laboratory) over a period of years was set in motion.

In 1970, Killian announced that the following year he would retire as chairman of the Corporation and that Johnson had been chosen to succeed him. In due course, Jerome Wiesner became president, Paul Gray, chancellor, and Walter Rosenblith, provost, the senior academic officer. With Johnson as chairman and Killian remaining as an active honorary chairman, the Institute had continuing strong leadership.

Sixty years after Jerry Hunsaker piloted M.I.T. into the Air Age, its engineers were probing outer space but were not finished with the problems of inner space. In the terminology of flight directors, the ceiling was still unlimited.

Two examples: The Department of Aeronautics and Astronautics had come up with a practicable method of disposing of atomic wastes by dumping them into the sun — a highly efficient incinerator safely 93,000,000 miles away but within reach of space vehicles. It was also wrestling with a more complex and defiant challenge to aeronautics — how to improve transportation on, or close to, the earth.

The fundamental technology for dealing with both problems had been developed. In relation to the value of electricity that can be generated in atomic power plants, the cost of dumping the dangerous garbage into the sun would be cheap, students found. And the clogging of urban arteries by the insistence of man on fast, convenient transportation can be cured by airbuses or other short-haul airplanes. The technology is by no means forbidding.

No field of engineering has been more innovative than that of aeronautics and astronautics. And no engineer more creative than Charles Stark Draper, who succeeded Hunsaker as head of the department in 1951. Strictly speaking, Draper is not an aeronautical engineer. He graduated from Stanford in psychology and received an S.B. in electrochemical engineering in 1926 from M.I.T., where he remained as a student for a dozen more years. The legend is that he took more courses than anyone else in the Institute's history and that he finally was given an ultimatum — make up your mind about your field and finish. He took an Sc.D. in physics.

Twenty years of study gave Draper a knowledge in science and engineering that he would use in later accomplishments. As an ROTC second lieutenant, he had gone to the Army Air Corps Flight School after graduation and qualified as a pilot. Returning to M.I.T. to work on a master's degree, he was an instructor in instrumentation and in his spare time did a lot of flying. His story of how he began developing inertial guidance goes like this: "Here I am in an airplane in the fog and I can't see a thing. I don't know where the hell I am or where I'm going. I don't know whether I'm right side up or wrong side up. I ask myself, 'If you can wear a wristwatch to tell you what time it is, why can't you have something that will tell you where you are with respect to space?' "

The answer lay in part in the gyroscope's ability to sense changes in altitude, and Draper conceived the idea of exploiting inertia for guidance. His student, Walter Wrigley '34, began working on a doctoral thesis on inertial guidance in 1938 and for years was his right-hand man and leading theoretician.

As we have seen, Draper applied the gyro to gun-pointing controls during World War II. When the postwar development of missiles started he was ready with ideas on how to guide them. His earliest system, FEBE, was first

36

Ceiling Unlimited

224

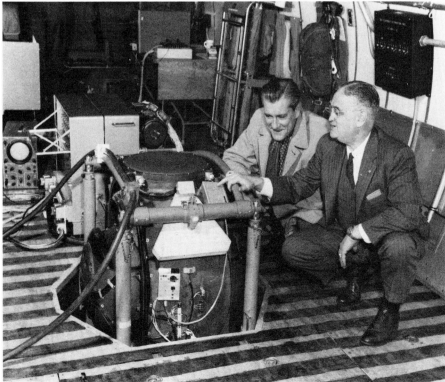

225

224   Charles Stark Draper had personal experience with three degrees of freedom in a flight trainer at Brooks Field in Texas while training as a pilot in 1926. Later he would use gimbals for more sophisticated purposes.

225   Draper demonstrated inertial guidance to Eric Sevareid on an unpiloted airplane flying to California. The first flight was made from Bedford, Massachusetts, to Los Angeles in 1953.

226   In the early days there were skeptics about inertial guidance, but probably no one ever doubted Draper's self-confidence.

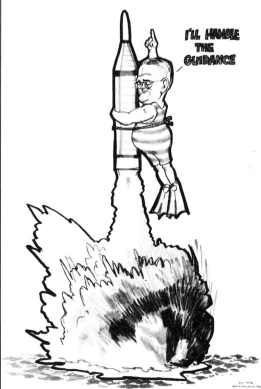

226

227

228

tested in 1949. More advanced systems followed. With gyros, accelerometers, servos, and electronics, an inertial guidance system could guide an airplane or missile or submarine with incredible accuracy.

SINS (for Submarine Inertial Navigation System) enabled submarines to cruise underwater anywhere in the world entirely free from outside reference. Inertial guidance for Polaris enabled them to launch this intercontinental ballistic missile from underwater with the certainty that it would reach its target. Draper's Poseidon system provided multiple nuclear weapons. For the Air Force, guidance systems were developed to use in Thor, Titan, and Sabre. Technology changed military strategy. And research on such systems increased the capacity of the Instrumentation Laboratory force — eventually more than two thousand people — to take on new projects.

Complex as all of the systems were, none was as elaborate and — in the public eye — as successful as the guidance and navigation system developed to take man to the moon. Very early Draper had envisioned ways of guiding vehicles into space. In the fifties his staff designed a robot to send to Mars, make pictures, and bring them back. (The project was rejected in favor of other ways to accomplish the mission.) When President Kennedy chose a landing on the moon as a national goal, NASA picked the Instrumentation Laboratory to design the Apollo guidance and navigation system.

227 In pre-Apollo times, psychologists predicted that the first person on the moon would be a Russian female midget with a Ph.D. in mathematics from M.I.T. — Russian because the Soviets were ahead in rocketry; a midget to squeeze into a small vehicle; female because a woman could better adapt to prolonged confinement; and an M.I.T. mathematician to deal with complex computer calculations.

228 As it turned out, one of the first two persons on the moon was an M.I.T. Sc.D. in Aeronautics and Astronautics, Edwin E. Aldrin Jr., a full-sized American male.

229

229   When Apollo 17, the last of the moon flights, successfully ended, Draper mounted a table with a glass of champagne to lead the laboratory staff in a celebration. At left with a cigar is Ralph R. Ragan '52, deputy director for NASA programs.

The guidance system was first tested in Apollo 3, an unmanned flight in 1966, and it worked beautifully in this and subsequent tests. When Apollo 11 was blasted up through the thunderclouds above Florida on July 16, 1969, Doc Draper and President Howard Johnson were there to watch and take satisfaction in its success. The pilot, Edwin E. "Buzz" Aldrin Jr. '63, was at the controls of the M.I.T.-designed system when the lunar module made the historic landing four days later and he was the second man to step to the powdery surface of the moon.

Through this and six subsequent missions, the revolutionary method of navigation did its job. The staff back at the Instrumentation Laboratory in Cambridge monitored all flights and when necessary made computer program modifications to deal with unexpected problems. In addition to Aldrin, three other M.I.T. alumni landed on the moon — Edgar D. Mitchell '64, on Apollo 14, David R. Scott '62, on 15, and Charles M. Duke Jr. '64, on 16. In addition, Russell L. Schweickart '56 was on Apollo 9, which orbited the moon. Three other alumni were among the Apollo astronauts who were trained, Anthony W. England '64, Philip K. Chapman '64, and William B. Lenoir '61. Before their flights, the assigned astronauts visited the Instrumentation Laboratory to familiarize themselves, in a training mockup, with the system.

Not only was Draper director of the Instrumentation Laboratory through this critical period but he was also head of the Department of Aeronautics and Astronautics until he reached retirement age in 1966. He continued as director of the laboratory until 1970, when it was spun off from M.I.T. and renamed the Charles Stark Draper Laboratory, of which he was president

230   231

230   Dr. Sheila Evans Widnall '60 joined the Aeronautics and Astronautics faculty in 1964, the first woman professor of engineering. In 1975 she went on leave to serve as the first director of the Office of University Research for the U.S. Department of Transportation. Her husband, William S. Widnall '59, formerly on the Instrumentation Laboratory staff, had an AIAA congressional fellowship to serve under the House Committee on Science and Astronautics.

231   Rene H. Miller, head of the Department of Aeronautics and Astronautics, has conducted extensive studies on the technology and economics of mass transportation by aircraft.

for two years. Draper was succeeded by Brigadier General Robert A. Duffy, who had been a special student at the laboratory two decades before.

Divorce of the laboratory did not mean that M.I.T. was withdrawing from space (and interaction of faculty and students with the Draper Lab continued). In 1963 an interdisciplinary Center for Space Research was organized as a framework within which scientists and engineers from Aeronautics and Astronautics and other departments could develop experiments.

Although the Department of Aeronautics and Astronautics was deeply involved in space and instrumentation, it had never lost interest in airplanes. Raymond L. Bisplinghoff, an authority on airframes who had served as director of the Office of Advanced Research and Technology for NASA, succeeded Draper as head of the department. He was succeeded in 1968 by Rene H. Miller, H. N. Slater Professor of Flight Transportation, who had been in the aircraft industry.

Miller has promoted space technology but his main interest, aside from presiding over a department of remarkably varied activities, has been in hunting for ways in which the airplane can reach its full potential in serving public needs. Why build expensive highways, which destroy the countryside and the city and which quickly become choked with polluting, fuel-wasting, uneconomical automobiles, when airplanes can transport people more rapidly and cheaply using the costless tracks through the air? That is his basic question.

Students and other faculty members have helped in studies to prove the economic feasibility of an extensive mass air transportation system and to develop the technology that is needed.

They are working on many other problems, such as new and pollution-free methods of propulsion; lighter, stronger, and safer airplanes; new types of space vehicles; and computer-controlled autopilots. Students have not yet given up on the construction of a human-powered "Burd" airplane to win an international prize as the first to fly one mile. (The craft they built cracked up in a taxi run in 1974 when a wing spar failed.) And among the present undergraduates there may be some who will fly far beyond the moon — though by brainpower, not musclepower.

37

M.I.T. Looks at the Cosmos

M.I.T. has never had a department of astronomy, and through most of its history it was rather aloof to the remote and inutile universe. Radar, radio, rocketry, and other Space Age developments have made it a leader in exploring the heavens.

Bruno Rossi is regarded as the father of the advance into astronomy in recent years. After beginning his cosmic ray research at the University of Florence in the twenties, he was forced to leave Italy and was invited to the University of Chicago by Arthur Compton. During World War II he worked at the Radiation Laboratory and at Los Alamos. He joined M.I.T. in 1945 and returned to research on cosmic rays, conducting observations in Colorado, Mexico, Bolivia, and elsewhere. He developed exquisitely fine instrumentation and trained many young scientists.

One of these students was Martin Annis '44, who became a research associate in physics and later founded a small Cambridge firm for research, American Science and Engineering, Inc., with Rossi as chairman of the board. Rossi and Riccardo Giacconi, who had joined the firm, sent up an X-ray scanner in an Aerobee rocket in 1962 and spotted the first observed X-ray source other than the sun — Sco X-1, which further research proved to be a faint blue star in the constellation Scorpio. Up to that time astronomers had supposed that X rays from stars would be too weak to detect. Sco X-1 was emitting a thousand times as much X radiation as visible light.

This discovery led to further search of the skies by rocket, balloon, and satellite. Since X rays and gamma rays are produced under cataclysmic conditions, they not only indicate the character of stars but may provide clues to cosmic evolution. Of special interest has been the Crab Nebula, which consists of remnants of the supernova — the stellar explosion — which the Chinese observed in A.D. 1054.

A continuous search for other X-ray sources was made possible by the launching of SAS-C (Small Astronomy Satellite C) in May of 1975 from San Marco Island, off the coast of Kenya. This all-M.I.T. satellite records X rays of various frequencies and transmits the data to an on-line computer at M.I.T. for analysis and storage. Optical observers are notified of discoveries

232   233

232   George Ellery Hale '90 was the greatest astronomer produced by M.I.T. and probably the greatest American astronomer of his time. For his bachelor's thesis he invented the spectroheliograph and with a telescope at Harvard made photographs of the sun's prominences. He built the Yerkes Observatory for the University of Chicago and then went to California as director of the Mount Wilson Observatory. He originated the idea and made possible the design and construction of the 200-inch Hale Telescope on Mount Palomar, completed in 1948, ten years after his death. He was the leader in building California Institute of Technology as a great institution.

233   Bruno Rossi's leadership in cosmic ray research was largely responsible for the emergence of M.I.T. in astronomy.

immediately so that they can train telescopes on X-ray sources — perhaps stars that had never seemed worth studying.

Launched by NASA's small Scout rocket, SAS-C was limited in size. More elaborate X-ray observations will be made for M.I.T. scientists by the HEAO (for High Energy Astronomical Observatory) series of 5,000-pound satellites to be sent into 300-mile orbits by Atlas-Centaur rockets starting in 1977.

These experiments are only a sample — but an important one — of exploration that has been conducted by the Center for Space Research since it was established in 1963. Among the most active of the two dozen professors who have participated in the research have been Hale V. Bradt '61, Herbert S. Bridge '50, George W. Clark '52, William L. Kraushaar, and Walter H. G. Lewin. Some four dozen students are engaged in research.

Among the subjects of continuing study has been the solar wind, first discovered by Rossi, Bridge, and others through observations by Explorer X, launched in 1961.

The application of radar to astronomy was begun in 1958 by Lincoln Laboratory when it started using its new Millstone Hill 84-foot antenna to probe the optically impenetrable atmosphere of Venus and later for radar mapping of the moon and Mars.

Sander Weinreb '58 devoted his bachelor's thesis to a study of how deuterium might be detected in interstellar space by radio astronomy and then, with Jerome Wiesner as his thesis adviser, he built an autocorrelation spectrometer for this purpose to qualify for a doctorate. Attempts at the National Radio Astronomy Observatory to detect deuterium were not successful, however.

Alan H. Barrett, a physicist, joined the faculty in 1961 and in 1963 he and Weinreb, who was then on the Lincoln Laboratory staff, along with

234

234   In 1950, M.I.T. researchers worked at the Inter-University High Altitude Laboratories in Colorado, making cosmic ray observations on 14,260-foot Mount Evans. Standing, left to right, are Martin Annis '44, Herbert Bridge '50, Ismael Escobar, Jerome J. Tiemann '53, and Daniel Anderson '52; kneeling, William Edgerton '55, Hans Courant '49, Robert Hewitt, and A. J. McMahon '51. Escobar, from the University of La Paz, returned to Bolivia and set up a station at 21,000 feet.

235   Since 1964 M.I.T. has been sending X-ray telescopes aloft on balloons to make observations each year. This one was launched in 1972 from Alice Springs, Australia, by a group headed by Walter H. G. Lewin.

236   The Haystack 120-foot dish, steerable within a rigid radome, has been enormously useful in radio and radar astronomy research. The man at the lower right gives an idea of its size.

235

236

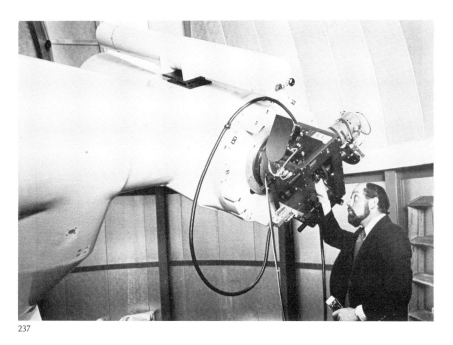

237

M. Littleton Meeks and John C. Henry of Lincoln, used the autocorrelation spectrometer at Millstone Hill, employing the 84-foot dish as a radio telescope, and succeeded in detecting hydroxyl — oxygen-hydrogen radicals in interstellar space.

Lincoln's Haystack Hill facility, with its 120-foot dish, started operating in 1963 and, being two thousand times as sensitive as Millstone, was capable of prodigious feats. Coupled with other radio telescopes, it has been used in what is known as VLBI, Very Long Baseline Interferometry. For instance, it was coordinated with a 72-foot Russian antenna in the Crimea to provide a 6,000-mile baseline for a study of nebulae as distant as 45 million light-years. Because of the Mansfield Amendment, Haystack was transferred to M.I.T. by the Air Force for use of the Northeast Radio Corporation, a consortium of a dozen institutions.

In spite of its increased activity in astronomy, M.I.T. still had no optical telescope until George R. Wallace Jr. '13 and his wife provided funds for the construction of an observatory just a mile from Haystack. Two telescopes, a computer-controlled 24-inch and an instructional 16-inch, were installed in 1971 and are operated by the Department of Earth and Planetary Sciences. The observatory is linked electronically with Haystack to permit simultaneous observations.

To provide access to a more powerful optical telescope, M.I.T. joined the University of Michigan and Dartmouth College to operate the 52-inch instrument that Michigan had been using near Ann Arbor. The telescope was moved in 1975 to Kitt Peak in Arizona, where the atmosphere is clearer and there is less interference from city lights. It became available in time to look at X-ray sources found by SAS-C.

238

239

For more than three centuries astronomers puzzled over the Great Red Spot on Jupiter — a spot as big as the entire surface of the earth. A plausible explanation for it finally was offered by two young M.I.T. professors, a meteorologist and a geochemist. The spot must be of red phosphorus produced by the action of ultraviolet light on phosphine in a sort of permanent hurricane on the turbulent and gassy planet.

Although laboratory experiments supported the hypothesis, proof is yet to come. In any case, the analysis provides an interesting example of Space Age collaboration between scientists from two departments which until a few years ago were concerned almost exclusively with rocks and weather on the earth. One of the scientists, Ronald G. Prinn of the Department of Meteorology, is still doing research on the earth's atmosphere. He has been seeking to determine whether nitrous oxide released by high-flying airplanes and Freon from aerosol cans will cut down the ozone and permit more harmful ultraviolet light to reach the earth's inhabitants. The reaction of Jupiter's atmosphere to ultraviolet is not unrelated.

The other scientist, John S. Lewis, is a geochemist in the Department of Earth and Planetary Sciences and he still gives attention to the earth, but he is among those who have found that a good way to study the earth is to study all of the planets and their moons. In fact, he has come up with a theory, the "equilibrium-condensation hypothesis," explaining why the primordial solar nebula could have given birth to planets of such different characteristics. This theory helps elucidate the structure and evolution of the earth.

At the time that William Barton Rogers founded M.I.T. and served as its first professor of geology, the idea of the evolution of the earth was as repugnant to some people as Darwinian theory. Rogers's study of the formation of the Appalachian Mountains had been a significant contribution to the scientific understanding of geological change.

Another professor of high scientific competence was William Otis Crosby '76, who was the first engineering geologist in the country and whose studies ranged from sulfur deposits in Mexico to gold mines in Alaska. He made geological surveys for his classmate, John R. Freeman, an eminent civil engineer, of the New York water system, the plan for creating the Charles River Basin, and the uncertain subsoil in Cambridge on which the new M.I.T. was to be built.

Geology was not established as a separate course at M.I.T. until 1890, previously having been offered as an option in "Natural History." Increasing attention was directed toward scientific research. Thomas A. Jagger Jr. set up a field station on the volcano Kilauea in Hawaii and, with the first continuous recording of seismic and volcanic activities, confirmed the relationship between the two in 1912. Waldemar Lindgren, a geologist of international reputation, published the authoritative book on the origin of mineral deposits. Hervey W. Shimer, long a member of the faculty — from 1903 to

38

Earth, Air, Oceans, and Beyond

240

1942 — and Robert R. Shrock compiled the definitive index to the fossils of North America, now in its ninth printing.

Martin J. Buerger '24 pioneered in crystallography, developing X-ray instrumentation and techniques to reveal the arrangement of atoms in a lattice. Patrick M. Hurley '40 extended comprehension of the earth's evolution through his geochemical research. His matching of rocks from Africa and Brazil, for example, demonstrated that the continents once were joined.

Development of plate tectonics — the study of movement of segments in the earth's crust — was the most significant advance in geology in more than a century. Essential evidence was to be found on the ocean floor, which involved oceanographic research. At the same time, many relationships of earth, sea, and air were becoming clearer. With this in mind, Shrock, then head of the Department of Geology and Geophysics, proposed a grouping of "Earth Sciences," with a closer relationship to the Department of Meteorology. Henry G. Houghton, head of the latter department, was equally interested. The Woods Hole Oceanographic Institution was delighted to join forces. And Shrock's friend Cecil H. Green, whose activities in oil exploration had been aided by M.I.T. talent, was interested to the point of providing a building for the Center for Earth Sciences. The joint program with WHOI, initiated in 1968, enables graduate students to attend classes in both Cambridge and Woods Hole and to study on research ships throughout the world. Joint degrees are given not only in earth sciences fields, such as marine geophysics, but also in biological oceanography and ocean engineering.

240   A glacial boulder was an interesting specimen for a geology field trip in western Massachusetts in the late nineteenth century. Fourth from the left, with a pick on his shoulder is George H. Barton '80, a professor from 1883 to 1904.

241

242

241   Students camped while attending the M.I.T. School of Geology, near Antigonish, Nova Scotia, which was operated in the summers from 1948 to 1961.

242   Robert R. Shrock, head of the Department of Geology for fifteen years, with Claude P. T. Hill '52 and Mrs. Donna G. Burt, technical assistant, examining fossil specimens.

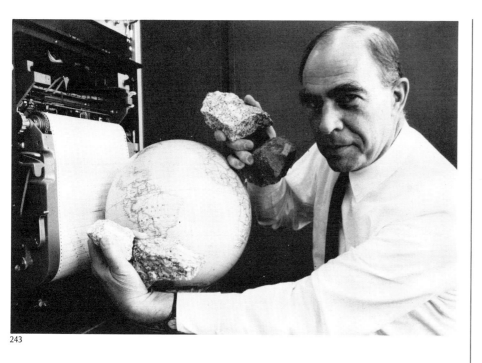

243

243   Patrick M. Hurley holds samples of matching rocks from Africa and Brazil, evidence that two continents were once joined. The samples were collected on an expedition organized by M.I.T. and the University of São Paulo.

244   M. Gene Simmons, geophysicist who served as chief scientist at the Manned Spacecraft Center when Apollo brought back rocks from the moon, prepares to subject a moon specimen to a pressure of 150,000 pounds per square inch to determine the velocity of sound in the rock at the equivalent to a 150-mile-deep pressure. Before the test he gets on the other side of the steel shielding in case of an explosion.

In 1965, Frank Press, director of the famed Seismological Laboratory at Caltech, became head of the Department of Geology and Geophysics and three years later its name was changed to Department of Earth and Planetary Sciences, indicating that its geological territory was now the entire solar system.

Press cooperated with Lincoln Laboratory in the seismic studies it was making with an enormous installation in Nebraska — LASA (for Large Aperture Seismic Array). With six hundred seismometers distributed over an area two hundred miles in diameter, this facility yielded information to permit discrimination between earthquakes and underground nuclear explosions — useful in negotiations toward a ban on underground nuclear tests and also useful in the detection of earthquakes. These and other studies, particularly of cracks and pores in rocks, have advanced the promise of earthquake prediction. In 1975, the George R. Wallace Jr. Geophysical Observatory, an underground seismic laboratory, was opened to give special attention to the prediction of earthquakes in New England, not as remote a possibility as is generally believed and of special importance in planning nuclear power plants. The new facility is adjacent to the department's Wallace Astrophysical Observatory, which helps gain knowledge of the solar system. Nearby is the big Haystack Observatory, which has been used for radar mapping of planets and which, as a radio antenna, will be used in determining the earth's plate movements with an expected accuracy of one centimeter a year.

Other pieces of information about the solar system are sent back by space vehicles cruising near the planets. Deep-diving submarines bring samples of

244

245

245   Frank Press, head of the Department of Earth and Planetary Sciences and Robert R. Shrock Professor of Geophysics, examines an earthquake rift in the Tadzhik Soviet Socialist Republic in 1973 while on a trip to work out a treaty with the Soviets setting up a protocol for an earthquake prediction program.

246   The Woods Hole Oceanographic Institution became available for research and education in a joint program with M.I.T. initiated in 1968. On the left side of the dock is *Lulu,* the twin-hulled mother ship for *Alvin,* deep-sea submarine. She is tied up astern of the *Knorr.* At right is the *Chain.*

246

basalt that has emerged from between plates in the Mid-Atlantic Ridge and deep-sea drilling produces cores of basement rock. A wealth of data is being obtained through a large number of projects.

In the Department of Meteorology, Henry M. Stommel, regarded as the world's leading authority on ocean circulation, led in conducting the Mid-Ocean Dynamics Experiment, an intensive survey of currents, temperatures, and other variables near Bermuda, in which sixteen institutions participated. The intimate relationship between ocean and atmosphere is illustrated in a finding by another professor, Erik L. Mollo-Christensen '48. He observed that "cat's paws," the ruffles on the water caused by light gusts, are involved in building up large waves. They enable the wind to get a "purchase" on the water. And that is why oil on troubled waters calms them. Experiments (with biodegradable oil) showed how a surface film smooths out the ripples.

Cat's paws are a tiny factor among myriad phenomena that make long-range forecasts so difficult. One member of the faculty, Edward N. Lorenz '43, is author of a widely accepted "theory of predictability," in which he demonstrated that even if all causes of weather patterns could be known (and they can't), prediction for more than a few weeks would be impossible.

Nevertheless, reliability in weather forecasting has increased. Predictions for two days are now as accurate as they were for one day twenty years ago, Jule G. Charney, head of the department, points out. Charney was a pioneer in the use of computers in the analysis of weather, having started his work with John von Neumann at the Institute for Advanced Study in Princeton back in the late forties. He continues to apply numerical methods to weather complexities. For instance, he has found that the aridity of areas around the Sahara Desert is related to the increased albedo — the increased reflectivity of the land — which has the effect of drying the air and reducing the capacity for rainfall. Satellite pictures indicate that overgrazing is a cause of the albedo's change. He is also conducting a study which may show that the Dust Bowl of the United States in the thirties was the product of that same process — overcultivation of the land.

247   In heavy seas in the Mediterranean, Bruce W. Larson, David L. Porter, and Harry L. Bryden (top to bottom), M.I.T. graduate students, retrieve a rosette sampler during a cruise aboard the *Chain* in early 1975. They were studying the conductivity and temperature of water at various depths.

247

If all the ships designed by M.I.T. alumni could be assembled, the fleet would reach as far as the eye could see. It would include practically all vessels built by the U.S. Navy in the last three-quarters of a century, for, beginning in 1901, Annapolis graduates destined to be ship constructors have been sent to M.I.T.

Included in the fleet would be a thousand or more boats built by Nathanael Herreshoff, one of the greatest American designers. He entered M.I.T. in 1866, its second year. As a boy in Rhode Island he had already become skillful and at the age of sixteen built a novel rotary steam engine. When President Rogers learned about the engine he asked Nat to demonstrate it before the Society of Arts.

Herreshoff left M.I.T. after three years and went into boatbuilding with his older brother, J. B. Herreshoff (who was blind). He designed and built the Navy's first torpedo boats, then the fastest in the world. He designed and built all the great yachts that defended the America's Cup between 1893 and 1920. After his brother's death in 1915 he sold the boatyard at Bristol, Rhode Island, and later it was operated by a group headed by Rudolf F. Haffenreffer '95.

39

As Broad as the Oceans

248

248   Nathanael G. Herreshoff of the Class of 1870, one of the greatest American naval architects.

Three of Herreshoff's sons graduated from M.I.T., A. Sidney deWolf Herreshoff '11, A. Griswold Herreshoff '12, and Nathanael Greene Herreshoff Jr. '12. Sidney's son, Halsey C. Herreshoff '60, was an instructor for four years and now has a partnership with his former professor, Justin E. Kerwin '53, in applying computer analysis to ship design. He served on three America's Cup defenders — *Columbia, American Eagle,* and *Courageous,* as navigator for the latter two. He has designed a number of yachts.

The Herreshoff story is only tangentially related to the history of nautical education and research at M.I.T. but indicates the tradition of achievement. The Department of Naval Architecture was founded in 1893 and offered the first course of its kind in the country. The founder was Cecil Hobart Peabody '77, a professor of mechanical engineeering and a stern disciplinarian. When the course for Annapolis graduates was inaugurated at M.I.T., William Hovgaard, a captain in the Danish navy and an authority on submarines, was recruited to take charge of it. Peabody was succeeded by another man of strong character, James Robertson Jack, a Scot who had worked for a shipyard in Dumbarton for thirty-eight years. Students joked that they had to learn two foreign languages — Danish and Scottish.

249   Third from the left is Cecil H. ''Peabo'' Peabody, first head of naval architecture, on a shipyard visit with students in 1901. To the right is Lydia G. Weld '02, the first woman to receive a degree in the field.

Like the shipbuilding industry, the department has had periods of boom and bust. Only nine graduates were in the Class of 1920. There was gradual growth after a new building, with "Pratt School of Naval Architecture and Marine Engineering" carved on its frieze, was erected in 1921 with a bequest left by George Herbert Pratt, a Boston lawyer.

For many years the department used the Charles River as a model basin for studies of hulls and propellors. A towing tank was installed in the Hydro-dynamics Laboratory when it was constructed in 1951. The tank was designed by its director, Martin A. Abkowitz '40, and has had a number of improvements, such as the installation of a wave generator controlled by magnetic tape, which can produce any kind of seas likely to be encountered by a ship.

During the final planning of the towing tank the head of the department was Rear Admiral Edward L. Cochrane '20, who during World War II was chief of the Navy's Bureau of Ships, supervising the greatest shipbuilding program in history. He went on leave in 1950 to serve as chairman of the Federal Maritime Board and administrator of the Federal Maritime Administration, and returned to M.I.T. to be dean of engineering and later vice-president.

Laurens Troost, director of the Netherlands Ship Model Basin, became head of the department in 1951. Later, for four years, H. Guyford Stever headed both naval architecture and mechanical engineering. He left to be president of Carnegie-Mellon University and then director of the National Science Foundation (and in that position, science adviser to the President). C. Richard Soderberg '20, former dean of engineering, served as head for a year and was instrumental in the selection of his successor, Alfred A. Keil, in 1966.

Having thrived under Scottish, Danish, Dutch, Swedish (Soderberg was born in Sweden), and other influences, the department experienced greater change under German direction than it ever had before. Keil, who received his doctorate from Friedrich Wilhelm University in 1939 and did research for the German Navy during the war, came to America in 1947 and was technical director of the Navy's David Taylor Model Basin in Washington.

A broader view of the oceans and their uses has been developing and Keil was charged with expanding the department's interests beyond the traditional one of building ships. The complexities of ocean usage required teaching and research in new shipping systems, harbor and port facilities, pollution, offshore oil drilling, continental shelf mining, fishing resources, and other areas. A year after Keil arrived the department began offering a new degree in "ocean engineering" and its name was changed in 1971 to the Department of Ocean Engineering. Another important development was the joint program with Woods Hole Oceanographic Institution, which made superb oceanographic facilities available.

In 1971, Keil became dean of engineering. He was succeeded as head of the department and director of the Sea Grant Program by Ira Dyer '49, a

250

250   The towing tank is machine-controlled and any size of waves can be generated for testing models.

251   Research at sea allows time for relaxation. This picture was made in 1968 during a cruise of the Woods Hole Oceanographic Institution research vessel *Gosnold*.

251

252

253

252   Lawrence A. Kahn '75, at the Maine laboratory, tests a water-driven underwater power tool in drilling a rock above water and gets as wet as if he were under water.

253   William A. Baker '34, a naval architect who became a historian and has served as curator of the Hart Nautical Museum since 1963. He prepared plans for reproduction of the *Mayflower* and other historic ships.

physicist and a specialist in underwater acoustics, indicating the extent to which departmental interests had broadened.

But teaching in naval architecture and marine engineering still accounts for 60 percent of the department's program. And in the Hart Nautical Museum, of which William A. Baker '34 is curator, it preserves the traditions of the seas, through the handsome fleet of model ships, in Nathanael Herreshoff's working drawings, and in many other marine treasures.

Although M.I.T. offered zoology and physiology from its beginning, there was no significant biology program until President Walker appointed William T. Sedgwick, one of his former students at Yale, as assistant professor of biology in 1883.

Sedgwick, who had started to study medicine at Yale and had gone to Johns Hopkins for a Ph.D. in physiology, was acutely aware of the poor preparation of medical students and conceived of biology at M.I.T. as a means of better pre-med education. Biology was established as a separate course in 1889 but few future medical students were attracted and the department came to be oriented toward public health.

There was much to be done in this area. William Nichols, Thomas Drown, and Ellen Richards had used chemical analysis in investigations of water pollution. Sedgwick added a knowledge of bacteria and has been called the father of epidemiology. (He was the founder and first president of the American Society of Bacteriologists.) When a dangerous typhoid epidemic struck Lowell and Lawrence, Massachusetts, he personally visited two thousand homes in tracking down sources of the disease — privies along the Merrimack River. He solved the problem with sand filtration for water supplies.

One of Sedgwick's students, George C. Whipple '89, who assisted him in research, became head of Harvard's Department of Sanitary Engineering. They were leaders in founding the Harvard-M.I.T. School for Public Health Officers in 1913. In 1922, the year of Sedgwick's death, Harvard assumed full responsibility for the school.

One of the first scientists to urge the pasteurization of milk, Sedgwick gave extensive attention to problems of food contamination. In 1895, William Lyman Underwood, grandson of the founder of Wm. Underwood Co., the oldest canners in the United States, came to Sedgwick for advice about spoilage problems. Sedgwick turned him over to his assistant, Samuel C. Prescott '94. Underwood was a prep school dropout and a maverick bored with the business details of canning but he had an intense interest in nature. He entered M.I.T. as a special student for one term and began a research partnership with Prescott that lasted for many years. They found that spoilage was caused by heat-resistant microorganisms and they worked out time-and-temperature tables that provided the scientific foundation for modern canning methods. The Underwood-Prescott Professorship of Food Science, the first endowed chair in food science in the United States, is a memorial to their collaboration. Samuel L. Goldblith '40 was selected as the first to hold it.

The Department of Food Technology was organized in 1945 and a new building, named in honor of John Thompson Dorrance '95, founder of Campbell's Soup, was built to house it and the Department of Biology. In postwar research, Bernard E. Proctor '23, head of Food Technology, and Goldblith, his deputy, pioneered in the use of ionizing energy in sterilizing foods.

40

Sciences of Life

254

255

256

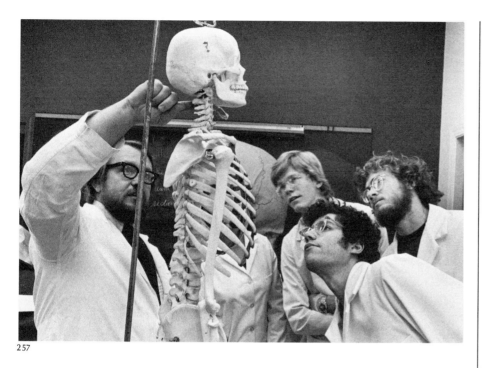

257

254 William T. Sedgwick with a biology class at about the turn of the century.

255 Samuel C. Prescott (center) conducted extensive research in the chemistry of coffee, invented the vacuum pack for it, and developed a new method of brewing. He used to say that he was promoted to dean of science because President Compton would smell the coffee and come to the laboratory, in Building 10, for a cup every day. At left are Robert Heggie '33, then a professor, and R. B. Woodward '36.

256 Gates-ajar collars and heavy suits were not inappropriate for dissecting an animal in the late nineteenth century. In the background are a skeleton and geological specimens, suggesting this may have been while the course was "Natural History."

257 In an anatomy class under D. W. Hamilton at Harvard Medical School are, left to right, David Scott Weigle, Allan S. Detsky, and Gilbert G. Berdine, among the hundred candidates for an M.D. degree in the Health Sciences and Technology Program.

258 Salvador Luria, Institute Professor and director of the Center for Cancer Research, who shared the Nobel Prize in 1969 for his discovery of mutations in viruses.

In 1961, Nevin S. Scrimshaw, who for a dozen years had been director of the Institute of Nutrition of Central America and Panama, was appointed head of the department and increasing attention was given to nutrition, the name being changed to Department of Nutrition and Food Science.

Meanwhile the Department of Biology had been undergoing spectacular transformation in a period of amazing advances in the understanding of viruses and of the DNA molecule, the pattern for the reproduction of all living things. Development in what was called molecular biology began with the appointment as head of the department in 1942 of Francis O. Schmitt, the first American researcher to apply X-ray diffraction and electron microscopy in this field. He took a special interest in the functioning of nerves and, in 1962, under the auspices of M.I.T., organized the Neurosciences Research Program as an international clearinghouse for brain research.

Irwin W. Sizer, who had pioneered in enzymology at M.I.T., became head of the department in 1957 and strengthened competence in biochemistry, of prime importance in molecular biology. He became dean of the Graduate School in 1967 and was succeeded by Boris Magasanik, a microbiologist. The same year, Robert A. Alberty, a chemist with a strong interest in chemical biology, was appointed dean of the School of Science.

M.I.T. activities related to health and the life sciences have been growing for many years. One important field has been that of the communications sciences, chiefly in communications biophysics and neurophysiology, centered in the Research Laboratory of Electronics. Norbert Wiener provided inspiration and mathematics for much of the early work. Jerome Wiesner, Walter Rosenblith, Warren S. McCulloch, and Jerome Y. Lettvin are among

258

259

259   Har Gobind Khorana, Alfred P. Sloan
Professor of Biology and Chemistry, who
shared the Nobel Prize in 1968, largely for
deciphering the genetic code and synthesis of
DNA.

those who have worked toward an understanding of communications
systems in man and other organisms.

This stream of research influenced another — the development of sensory
aids for the blind and of various prosthetic devices. A central figure has been
a mechanical engineer, Robert W. Mann '50, who is Uncas A. Whitaker
Professor of Biomedical Engineering. Applying the ideas of Norbert Wiener,
for example, he was a codeveloper of the "Boston Arm," an artificial arm
that is controlled electronically by the bioelectrical signals generated in the
muscles of the wearer.

Such interest in medically related problems (and scores of other examples
could be given) resulted in the establishment in 1970 of the Program in Health
Sciences and Technology by M.I.T. and Harvard. The Harvard Medical School
and related hospitals, the School of Public Health, and the Division of Engineering and Applied Physics cooperate with more than a dozen M.I.T.
departments in research. The joint program is one of the most important
in which M.I.T. has ever become engaged, providing means to apply modern
science and technology to health problems and to develop new kinds of
physicians and health scientists.

Partly because of their own experience in medically related communications sciences, Jerome Wiesner and Walter Rosenblith led in developing the

260

260 The "Ergograph," used in a study of fatigue in the Physiological Laboratory early in the century. With his hand strapped down, the researcher pulled a spring scale with one finger, registering the amount of work done on a revolving smoked drum at the left.

261 The Boston Arm is activated by bio-electrical signals in the muscles of an amputee. It was developed by Robert W. Mann and others on the basis of ideas advanced by Norbert Wiener.

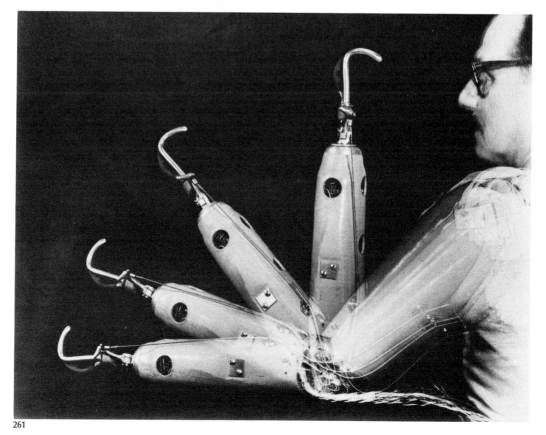

261

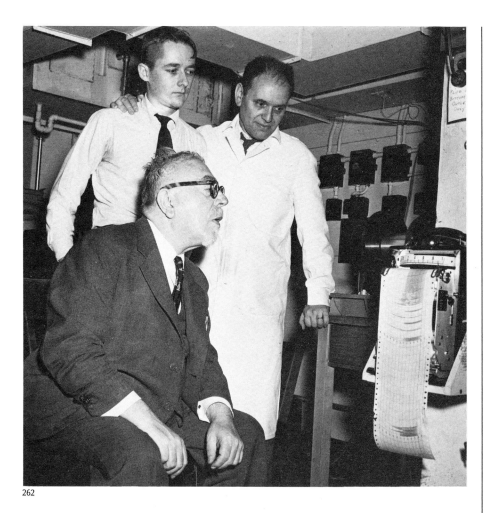

262

262   Norbert Wiener worked with Walter A. Rosenblith (right), now Institute Professor and provost, and John Barlow of Massachusetts General Hospital in computer analysis of brain waves and found significant patterns not detected before, including evidence of a timing device.

263   Nevin S. Scrimshaw, head of the Department of Nutrition and Food Science, has been a leader in seeking solutions to world problems of undernourishment.

program — Wiesner as provost and then president; Rosenblith as chairman of the faculty and then as provost. In the latter position, Rosenblith has the responsibility for the HST program, along with more than a score of other projects and divisions.

One of the many aspects of the HST program is that a hundred students working toward the M.D. degree at Harvard Medical School are able to take courses at M.I.T. in preparation for special fields. A cardiologist, for instance, can become well grounded in electrical engineering and a neurologist can establish a foundation in the neural behavioral sciences.

Sedgwick's hope that a scientific education could be offered to pre-med students at M.I.T. is being realized even better than he could have hoped. In various fields, but especially in biology, an increasing number of M.I.T. graduates have been going to medical schools — about a hundred each year.

Another outstanding example of M.I.T.'s commitment to medically related research was the establishment in 1973 of the Center for Cancer Research, directed by Salvador E. Luria, who was awarded the Nobel Prize for his research on viruses. The program of the center is devoted to fundamental

263

studies of cancer biology. One of the researchers is David Baltimore '61, who holds the American Cancer Society Professorship of Microbiology. He identified an enzyme in certain viruses that produce cancers in animals and is working with other virologists to determine the mechanisms by which viruses cause cells to act as cancer cells. He shared the Nobel Prize for medicine-physiology in 1975.

The Center for Cancer Research is located in the Seeley G. Mudd Building, which was dedicated in 1975, along with facilities for the Health Sciences and Technology and other biomedical programs.

41
Quest
for
Learning

"**W**e are all gathered here, teachers and students, to expand man's knowledge of the universe. No doctrine, no orthodoxy, no conventional discipline or gust of political passion can be allowed to divert us from this purpose."

The gusts of political passion had not entirely subsided as Jerome B. Wiesner made this statement at his inauguration as president of M.I.T. on October 7, 1971. He was appealing for scholarly tranquillity and also affirming his belief in the basic purpose of a university — "the quest for learning, the nurture of learning, the transmission of learning, the use of learning."

Then fifty-six years old, Jerry Wiesner had spent nearly half his life dealing with large-scale problems. His last duty at the Radiation Laboratory was as project engineer for Project Cadillac — development of an extremely complex electronics system that would enable the military command to watch (by radar) and coordinate fleets of ships and airplanes in the monstrous assault on Japan. When the atomic bomb canceled that plan, he became leader of an electronics group at Los Alamos.

Through the 1950s, while director of the Research Laboratory of Electronics, Wiesner participated in a number of summer studies on large defense problems, and he was increasingly concerned about the biggest problem of all — how to prevent war. He was staff director of the U.S. delegation to the Geneva Conference for the Prevention of a Surprise Attack, in 1958. As science adviser to President John F. Kennedy and then President Lyndon B. Johnson, from 1961 to 1964, he was deeply involved in momentous matters, such as achieving the Nuclear Test Ban Treaty.

But Wiesner had never lost interest in education. At the White House he was responsible, for instance, for important studies of education by panels under the President's Science Advisory Committee — both of them chaired by M.I.T. professors, Edwin Gilliland and Jerrold Zacharias. He had intimate knowledge of educational issues at M.I.T. As a young professor he had worked on the policy-shaping Lewis Report. As acting head of the Department of Electrical Engineering before he went to Washington and dean of the School of Science and then provost after his return, he had heavy educational responsibilities.

Teamed with President Wiesner, Chancellor Paul E. Gray was equally concerned with education and had been a leader in curriculum reform for more than a decade. He had served as chairman of the Freshman Advisory Council, associate dean of student affairs, associate provost, and dean of engineering. Wiesner and Gray faced many pressing problems, the most enormous being what was sometimes called "The Cash Crunch." The Institute's costs were going up faster than its income from regular sources, and if it was to continue to make progress in education and research, massive new funding would be required. With Howard W. Johnson and Paul F. Hellmuth '47, a prominent Boston attorney, as cochairmen, a five-year campaign for $225,000,000 was announced in 1975. The amount was large, but so was the need for augmentation of the endowment, for support of professorships, for student loans and scholarships, for new facilities and other purposes.

Johnson, Wiesner, Gray, and thousands of alumni would be very busy if the "M.I.T. Leadership Campaign" were to succeed. Meanwhile there must be progress toward less tangible goals within the Institute. High priority was given to educational problems. Ever since the Lewis Report, faculty and students had sought ways to improve the curriculum and processes of learning. There was general credence in the tradition of rigor, of high standards. (Though the most extreme of student dissidents would have abolished entrance and graduation requirements, grades, examinations, degrees, and perhaps the faculty.) How to maintain that tradition and yet make education as exciting as it should be, in preparation for the creative, socially constructive life of the individual, was the crux of the problem.

Back in 1957, Edwin H. Land, the genius who invented the Polaroid camera, had given the Arthur Dehon Little Memorial Lecture at M.I.T., titled "Generation of Greatness," which had continuing impact on the thinking about education at M.I.T. He believed that the standard university system of examinations and grading served to stifle the potential of students for greatness. Rather than being treated as immature boys, they should be accepted by professors as young colleagues and immediately be given opportunities for independent, stimulating research. A few years later, Land (who within his Polaroid Corporation was experimenting with educational innovation) set up a trust fund for M.I.T. to use, and this was drawn upon as one source of funding for an especially significant undertaking — UROP, the Undergraduate Research Opportunities Program.

This program, inaugurated in 1969, was directed to discovery of research projects that students could undertake outside the curriculum, the sort of thing that Land hoped could be done. Under the leadership of Margaret L. A. MacVicar '64, an energetic young physics professor, it grew until half of the undergraduates and half of the faculty were participating in any one

264

264   President and Mrs. Wiesner (center) greeted students and faculty at a reception in the Great Court following his inauguration. At right is Mrs. Carolyn Cox, director of the Registry of Guests.

265   Contributions made by the wives of the last five presidents to the agreeable tone of campus life — often quietly and in ways that were not generally apparent — have been enormous. From the right, they are Mrs. Margaret Compton, Mrs. Elizabeth Killian, Mrs. Catherine Stratton, Mrs. Elizabeth Johnson, and Mrs. Laya Wiesner.

265

266

266   At the same time that Jerome Wiesner
was elected president, Paul E. Gray (left) was
elected by the Corporation as chancellor and
deputy to the president. Both have served
as professors of electrical engineering and both
have qualified to be regarded, in the broadest
sense of the term, as educators.

semester. Furthermore, students were invited to take over projects in companies or other institutions. Massachusetts General Hospital, for example,
wanted a student to research materials for artificial lungs, and a New Orleans
firm asked for one to test and improve a machine for picking crab meat.

In his enthusiasm for UROP, Paul Gray recalled his own experience as an
undergraduate — how he was turned on by a one-to-one relationship with
a young electrical engineering professor, Thomas F. Jones Jr. '40. He got a
job in the laboratory to earn money but suddenly discovered he was being
educated.

As a professor, Gray himself was an innovator. In 1961, he, Richard B.
Adler '43, Campbell L. Searle '51, and Richard D. Thornton '54 deplored the
fact that vacuum tube technology was still being taught at a time when solid
state was beginning to dominate electronics. They led in the formation of
the Semiconductor Electronics Education Committee for curricular revision
throughout the country.

Jerrold Zacharias has doubtless been the most conspicuous educational
reformer at M.I.T. In the late fifties he was the driving force behind the
Physical Science Study Committee, which revolutionized the teaching of
physics in American high schools. With the help of President Killian and
others, he pushed reform into various fields through an independent agency,
Educational Services, Inc. This nonprofit organization eventually became the
Educational Development Center, Inc., which is active internationally in
making films and applying educational innovation in other ways.

Zacharias was one of the sparks behind radical changes in the teaching
of physics and other subjects at M.I.T. In 1962 he was appointed by President
Stratton as chairman of a Committee on Curriculum Content Planning, which

was extremely influential. He was closely associated with Francis L. Friedman '49 in the formation of the Science Teaching Center for educational investigation, and when Friedman — still in his youth — died, Zacharias carried on the work.

This center — later called the Education Research Center — provided the initiative in a variety of innovations, such as the Unified Science Study Program, permitting students to do concentrated work rather than follow the conventional plan.

M.I.T. has shown no inclination to establish a school of education, but many of its people have demonstrated competence in educational research and invention. Recognizing this, President Wiesner in 1973 created the Division for Study and Research in Education. The first director was William Ted Martin, long-time head of the Department of Mathematics. In 1975 Provost Rosenblith announced his successor to be Benson R. Snyder, who came to M.I.T. as psychiatrist in chief, became fascinated with the problems of education, and wrote a provocative book, *The Hidden Curriculum*. Such people as Zacharias and Judah L. Schwartz, a physicist who had been active in the Education Research Center, joined the staff. Gray's old preceptor, Tom Jones, after more than a decade as president of the University of South Carolina, returned as a visiting professor in the division (and in 1975 was appointed as the Institute's vice-president for research).

The old notion was that anyone who was an expert in his field would be a good university teacher. Research has shown that there are many subtleties in the processes of teaching and learning that are vital in education, and that their full understanding is yet to be achieved. The division is probing deep into the philosophy of pedagogy and cognition, with an interdisciplinary approach that touches on psychology, anthropology, and other fields.

The division is interested not only in education at M.I.T. and at the college level. One of the staff members, Seymour A. Papert, has been conducting research with children in the Artificial Intelligence Laboratory. (The intelligence of computers is artificial — not that of children.) Much of his experimentation has centered on use of a computer-controlled robot — the Turtle, an electronic device that can be directed to draw geometrical figures or even pictures. Children love to "play" with the Turtle, and in the process of operating the computer they learn how to think; furthermore, they reveal *how* they think. Out of such research, Papert believes there will come a deeper understanding of the human mind and better ideas on how to help in learning.

One of President Wiesner's associates believes his outstanding characteristic is his intuitive ability "to think what you haven't thought of." Or, in other words, "to see a problem in its wholeness and to have a creative insight into how to resolve it."

There is no single, simple objective of education at M.I.T., but disciplined creativeness is becoming more highly prized. Let Turtles do the drudgery; let people do the thinking.

267

268

269

267   The Turtle, a computer-controlled robot which draws pictures, is used by Seymour Papert in teaching and exploring the processes of learning. Children become entranced with the problems of using logic to direct the Turtle's movements.

268   A spelling bee would have been thought hopelessly quaint by some generations of college students, but in 1975 Kresge Auditorium was jammed with an audience to watch fifty contestants try for the championship. The fifty were chosen from 210 who took a preliminary test. The winner was Norman M. Brenner, a graduate student in the Department of Earth and Planetary Sciences.

269   Universities are sometimes accused of turning out students on assembly lines. At M.I.T., a more appropriate metaphor is provided by the unicycle. Accomplishment depends on individual effort and dexterity. And professors have observed an increasing penchant for educational risk-taking — for choosing difficult challenges rather than taking the easy, prosaic way.

"Tech didn't welcome its incoming classes then — it challenged them," wrote John W. Rockefeller Jr. '20 of his arrival as a freshman.

"There was not a tree or blade of grass in the great court — nothing but acres of crushed stone and the temporary unpainted wooden walks traversing them. It was a sight that in less than two years would make the brick barracks of Fort Monroe seem warm and homelike by comparison."

The look — and the character — of M.I.T. have changed a great deal since that time. In 1928 the court was landscaped and, with its rhododendrons and elms, it has grown more beautiful ever since. In 1974 it was named Killian Court in honor of James R. Killian Jr., who referred to it as an "oasis of beauty and serenity." Other such oases have been created.

But the change goes deeper than landscaping, which is one of its manifestations. In the same way that there has always been excitement about science and technology, there is excitement about the arts — all of them — poetry, music, dance, drama; visual, literary, performing, decorative, cinematic, photographic. And this excitement does not represent merely a thirst for "culture" but a widespread conviction that the arts are a profoundly important part of life; that a sonnet or a sonata can be as significant as a Schrödinger equation.

The Department of Architecture since its early days has been a torchbearer for the arts and for more than two decades the Department of Humanities has been the main protagonist for the arts other than visual. Both have set high standards in professionalism of their creative staff members. Architecture was the parent of the Center for Advanced Visual Studies, organized by Gyorgy Kepes as a place where practicing artists could work together in advanced projects, especially those related to science and technology.

An influence of special importance in recent years has been the view that the arts should involve the total environment, that they should be enjoyed and participated in by many, not a privileged few; that they can contribute to public festival. During a recent year some three hundred art events were held at M.I.T. with a total audience estimated at 100,000.

In 1971 President Wiesner announced the formation of an M.I.T. Council for the Arts, a "catalyst for development of a broadly based, highly participatory, widely ranging program that is firmly founded on teaching, practice and research in the arts." He said, "We hope eventually to transform M.I.T. into a large multi-purpose arts center."

Speaking later at a meeting of the Council, Wiesner said: "I happen to believe that the arts are in fact 'useful' knowledge and that the imagination, the mental muscle of man's spirit, atrophies if it is not used. We do not yet have the facts and configurations to prove that the arts are useful, but I do suspect it is susceptible to proof and I think it will probably need to be proved if society is to take cultural development seriously."

42

No Atrophy of Imagination

270

271

270   Welles Bosworth envisioned the temple-like Rogers Building lobby as having statues in the four corners, and pedestals were provided for them. Christopher Wren would have been in the southwest.

271   In recent years, students — especially those in architecture — have regarded the Rogers lobby as not just a place to pass through but as one of community interaction. Elaborate experimental structures have been built and performances have included nearly everything except an elephant act. In this one, Gustave M. Solomons Jr. '61, architecture graduate who became a dancer, leads his group.

272

272   "Balloon Carpet" was the title of this creation by Otto Piene in 1974, filmed in the Rogers lobby for German television.

273   Otto Piene, Gyorgy Kepes (who was then director of the Center for Advanced Visual Studies), and Harold Tovish, then a fellow at the center, with a model for a huge construction projected for Boston Harbor.

274   Robert O. Preusser (right), professor of visual design, and Andres Schcolnik, an artist, adjust lights for an exhibition titled "Lightworks" at the Hayden Gallery in 1973. The show presented experiments by fourteen of Preusser's students in the use of lasers and other technical devices to create visual experiences in a darkened gallery. Preusser is on the Architecture faculty but his students come from many other departments and use various technical skills in creative studies.

273

274

275

276

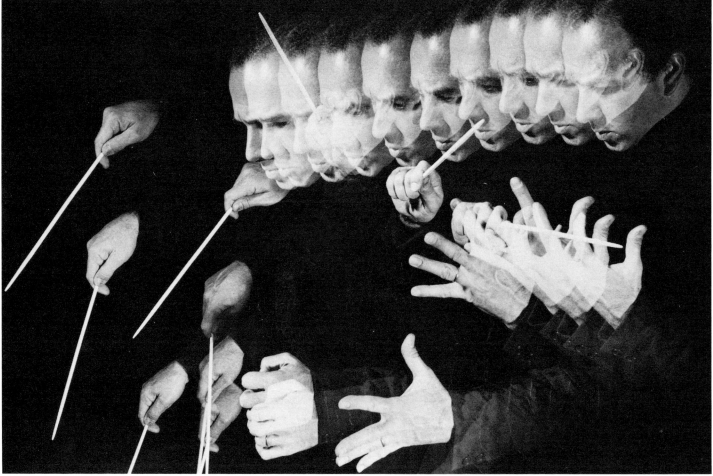

277

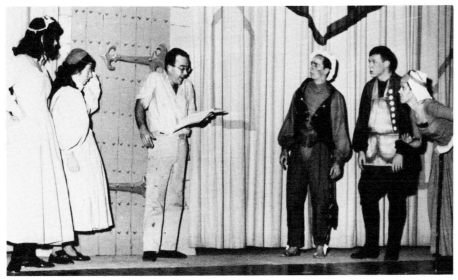

278

279

275   Luis A. Ferré '24, then president-elect of the M.I.T. Alumni Association, was back in 1974 for an exhibition at the Hayden Gallery of 36 paintings from the Museo de Arte de Ponce, which he founded. Former governor of Puerto Rico, he is a member of the M.I.T. Corporation and the Council for the Arts.

276   Janet Stober '64 played the Beethoven Violin Concerto with the M.I.T. Symphony in 1963, reported by *The Tech* as "a truly breath-taking performance."

277   David Epstein, photographed by mul-tiple flash by Charles E. Miller of the Strobo-scopic Laboratory, is not only conductor of the M.I.T. Symphony but a distinguished violist and composer.

278   Joseph Everingham, professor of litera-ture and director of drama, has maintained high standards for student productions. Here he rehearses the cast of Ben Jonson's *Bartholomew Fair*.

279   Through the efforts of President Wiesner, M.I.T. acquired in 1975 a concrete sculpture conceived by Pablo Picasso. Titled *Figure découpée*, it was executed by Carl Nesjar, a Norwegian artist who was formerly a fellow at the Center for Advanced Visual Studies. An anonymous donor made possible the acquisition of the sculpture by the M.I.T. Committee on the Visual Arts. Workmen are shown removing supporting timbers after installing it outside the Hermann Building.

Most of the fifty-four original incorporators of M.I.T., who met in 1862 for the first annual meeting of the Institute's "Government," were Bostonians. Today the Corporation, as the governing body is known, includes members from many parts of the United States and from abroad. Their backgrounds are varied but most are distinguished leaders in industry, science, education, the professions, and public service. They have one thing in common — an interest in devoting time to the service of the Institute. M.I.T. has a tradition of active, not passive, trusteeship.

The Corporation has seventy-five members. One-third of the active membership are life members. Two-thirds serve for five-year renewable terms. Twenty of the term memberships are filled by alumni, selected by alumni, and the president of the Alumni Association is an ex-officio member. The governor of Massachusetts, the chief justice of the Supreme Judicial Court, and the commissioner of education also serve ex-officio as representatives of the Commonwealth. The Executive Committee of the Corporation maintains a month-to-month involvement in the Institute's affairs and the Investment Committee has continuing oversight of investment policy.

Of all Corporation members, about 85 percent are alumni. The first alumnus to be a member was Howard A. Carson '69, who was elected in 1878 and served for fifty-three years — longer than any other member. Over the years there have been a number of bylaw changes that increased the number of alumni on the Corporation. The controversy of 1905 over the proposed merger with Harvard resulted in a bylaw amendment that gave alumni a numerical majority on the Corporation for the first time.

In 1970, provision was made for five alumni as representatives of recent classes. The first alumna elected was Dr. Mary Frances Wagley '47, headmistress of St. Paul's School for Girls in Maryland. The first black American member, elected in 1969, is Jerome H. Holland, former ambassador to Sweden. The first European was William R. Hawthorne '39, distinguished British engineer, and the first South American, Virgilio Barco '43, a senator in Colombia.

One of the ways in which Corporation members serve the Institute is participation in Visiting Committees, which periodically examine twenty-eight departments, laboratories, and other activities. These committees include members of the Corporation and a total of more than 350 scientists, engineers, educators, and executives.

Another important activity is that of the Corporation Development Committee, which includes twenty-five Corporation members and more than 125 alumni. This committee, with a total membership of 150, meets regularly with the Corporation to advise and plan in resource development of the Institute.

The Corporation Joint Advisory Committee on Institute-Wide Affairs was established in 1970 to provide a forum for the discussion of issues by Corporation members, students, and faculty.

43

The Corporation

280   Members of the M.I.T. Corporation present for the 1974 annual meeting were, left to right: *seated,* Lloyd D. Brace, Thomas D. Cabot, Cecil H. Green, Edward J. Hanley, John J. Wilson, Julius A. Stratton, Paul E. Gray, Jerome B. Wiesner, Howard W. Johnson, James R. Killian Jr., Joseph J. Snyder, Marshall B. Dalton, Donald F. Carpenter, William A. Coolidge, David A. Shepard, James B. Fisk, and Walter J. Beadle.
Second row: George P. Gardner Jr., Uncas A. Whitaker, Pamela T. Whitman, Luis A. Ferré, W. Gerald Austen, Mary F. Wagley, Irénée du Pont Jr., Virgilio Barco, William S. Brewster, Ralph M. Davison, Cecily C. Selby, John C. Haas, Frank R. Milliken, Rebecca A. Donellan, William S. Edgerly, J. Kenneth Jamieson.
Third row: Kenneth H. Olsen, Jerome H. Holland, George W. Thorn, Robert B. Semple, Paul V. Keyser, Ralph Landau, James A. Champy, I. M. Pei, Paul P. Shepherd, Angus N. MacDonald, Charles B. McCoy, Philip H. Peters, Gregory Smith, James E. Turner, Edward O. Vetter.
Fourth row: Charles E. Reed, Breene M. Kerr, Carl M. Mueller, Sekazi K. Mtingwa, Laurence Storch, Louis W. Cabot, Frank T. Cary, Thomas F. Creamer, Edward E. David Jr.

Not included in the photograph are: Gregory Anrig, Gregory C. Crisholm, W. Van Alan Clark Jr., Paul M. Cook, Bradley Dewey, Russell DeYoung, James H. Doolittle, W. H. Krome George, Crawford H. Greenewalt, Robert C. Gunness, Semon E. Knudsen, George J. Leness, Alfred L. Loomis, Robert A. Lovett, Ralph Lowell, H. W. McCurdy, Clint W. Murchison Jr., William B. Murphy, Ellmore C. Patterson, Gwilym A. Price, Laurance S. Rockefeller, Francis W. Sargent, Robert C. Sprague, G. Joseph Tauro, Charles A. Thomas, Jeptha H. Wade, D. Reid Weedon Jr., and Irving W. Wilson.

The following were elected to the Corporation in 1975: Vernon E. Jordan Jr., Norman B. Leventhal, Wilfred D. MacDonnell, Allan J. MacEachen, Harold J. Muckley, William J. Weisz, and Shirley A. Jackson. Howard L. Richardson, elected president of the Alumni Association for 1975–1976, began a one-year term as an ex-officio member.

Bibliography

Babson, Roger W. *Actions and Reactions, An Autobiography*. New York: Harper & Brothers, 1935.

Baker, William A. *A History of the First 75 Years*. Cambridge: M.I.T., Department of Naval Architecture and Marine Engineering, 1969.

Baxter, James Phinney, III. *Scientists Against Time*. Boston: Little, Brown, 1946.

Bigelow, Jacob. *Elements of Technology*. Boston: Hilliard, Gray, Little and Wilkins, 1829.

Bone, Alexander J., and George E. Russell. "History of the Civil Engineering Department, M.I.T." Unpublished ms.

Bruce, James L. *The Rogers Building and Huntington Hall*. Boston: Proceedings of the Bostonian Society, 1941.

Bruce, Robert V. *Bell*. Boston: Little, Brown, 1973.

Burchard, John E., and Albert Bush-Brown. *The Architecture of America*. Boston: Little, Brown, 1961.

————, ed. *Mid-Century; the Social Implications of Scientific Progress*. Cambridge: M.I.T. Press, 1950.

————. *Q.E.D. — M.I.T. in World War II*. Cambridge: Technology Press, 1948.

Burgess, F. Gelett. *The Purple Cow and Other Nonsense*. New York: Dover Publications, 1961.

Bush, Vannevar. *A Keepsake in Honor of Vannevar Bush*. Cambridge: M.I.T. Press, 1959.

————. *Modern Arms and Free Men*. New York: Simon & Schuster, 1949.

————. *Pieces of the Action*. New York: William Morrow, 1970.

Carr, William H. A. *The Du Ponts of Delaware*. New York: Dodd, Mead, 1964.

Clarke, Robert. *Ellen Swallow*. Chicago: Follett Publishing Co., 1964.

Compton, Arthur H. *Atomic Quest*. New York: Oxford University Press, 1956.

Compton, Karl T. *A Scientist Speaks*. Cambridge: M.I.T. Undergraduate Association, 1955.

Conant, James B. *My Several Lives*. New York: Harper & Row, 1970.

Cross, Charles R. *Early History of the Alumni Association of the Massachusetts Institute of Technology*. Cambridge: Technology Press, 1920.

Danzig, Allison. *Oh, How They Played the Game*. New York: Macmillan, 1971.

Deutsch, Karl W., John Platt, and Dieter Senghaas. "Conditions Favoring Advances in Social Science." *Science*, February 5, 1971.

Du Pont. Wilmington: E. I. du Pont de Nemours & Company, 1952.

Dutton, William S. *Du Pont*. New York: Charles Scribner's Sons, 1942.

Flexner, Abraham. *Henry S. Pritchett*, New York: Columbia University Press, 1943.

Gurney, A. R., Jr. *The Gospel According to Joe*. New York: Harper & Row, 1974.

Harrison, George R. "Karl Taylor Compton." Unpublished ms.

————. *What Man May Be*. New York: William Morrow, 1956.

Herreshoff, L. Francis. *Capt. Nat Herreshoff*. New York: Sheridan House, 1953.

Hodgins, Eric. *Trolley to the Moon*. New York: Simon & Schuster, 1973.

Holman, Silas W. "Massachusetts Institute of Technology." Chapter XIII in *Higher Education in Massachusetts*. Washington, D.C.: U.S. Government Printing Office, 1889.

Hunt, Caroline L. *The Life of Ellen H. Richards*. Boston: Whitcomb and Barrows, 1912.

James, Henry. *Charles W. Eliot*. Boston: Houghton Mifflin, 1930.

Jones, Howard Mumford. *Primer of Intellectual Freedom*. Cambridge: Harvard University Press, 1949.

Jordan, E. O., G. C. Whipple and C.-E. A. Winslow. *A Pioneer in Public Health, William Thompson Sedgwick*. New Haven: Yale University Press, 1924.

Kahn, E. J., Jr. *The World of Swope*. New York: Simon & Schuster, 1965.

Kane, Henry B. *M.I.T. in the Twenties.* Cambridge: M.I.T. Alumni Association, 1968.

Killian, James R., Jr. *A Record of the Writings and Addresses and Excerpts from the Presidential Inaugural Address.* Cambridge: M.I.T. Press, 1971.

————. *Cambridge (Mass.) University.* Unpublished ms. presented before the Examiner Club, 1952.

————. "Good Neighbor Policy in Cambridge." *Technology Review,* November 1951.

————. "Vannevar Bush." Unpublished address at a memorial service, 1974.

Laurence, William L. *Men and Atoms.* New York: Simon & Schuster, 1959.

Lee, Calvin B. T. *The Campus Scene: 1900–1970.* New York: David McKay, 1970.

Lewis, Arthur L. *The Day They Shook the Plum Tree.* New York: Harcourt, Brace & World, 1963.

The Lewis Story. A Dollar to a Doughnut. Privately printed, 1953.

Logsdon, John M. *The Decision to Go to the Moon.* Cambridge: MIT Press, 1970.

Luria, S. E. *Life — The Unfinished Experiment.* New York: Scribner's, 1973.

Margulies, Rebecca Zames, and Peter M. Blau. "America's Leading Professional Schools." *Change,* November 1973.

————. "The Reputations of American Professional Schools." *Change,* Winter 1974–75.

Marks, Percy. *The Plastic Age.* New York: The Century Co., 1924.

M.I.T. *Technology's War Record, 1914–1919.* War Records Committee.

M.I.T. *The War Record,* 1945.

M.I.T. Radiation Laboratory. *Five Years.* Cambridge: M.I.T., 1946.

Morison, Elting E. *From Know-How to Nowhere.* New York: Basic Books, 1974.

————. *Turmoil and Tradition.* Boston: Houghton Mifflin, 1960.

Munroe, James Phinney. *A Life of Francis Amasa Walker.* New York: H. Holt, 1923.

Nicholson, Natalie N. "The Massachusetts Institute of Technology Libraries." Ms. for Encyclopedia of Library and Information Science, 1974.

Ober, Shatswell, *The Story of Aeronautics at M.I.T., 1895–1960.* Cambridge: M.I.T. Department of Aeronautics and Astronautics, 1965.

Papert, Seymour. *Uses of Technology to Enhance Education.* Cambridge: M.I.T. Artificial Intelligence Laboratory, 1973.

Pearson, Henry Greenleaf. *Richard Cockburn Maclaurin.* New York: Macmillan, 1937.

Pioneering in Aeronautics. Recipients of Daniel Guggenheim Medal. New York: Board of Award, 1952.

Prescott, Samuel C. *When M.I.T. Was "Boston Tech."* Cambridge: Technology Press, 1954.

R.L.E.: 1946 + 20. M.I.T. Research Laboratory of Electronics, 1966.

Richards, Robert Hallowell, His Mark. Boston: Little, Brown, 1936.

Rockefeller, John W., Jr. *The Poor Rockefellers.* New York: Vanguard Press, 1962.

Rogers, William Barton, Life and Letters, Edited by His Wife. Boston: Houghton Mifflin, 1896.

Rosenblith, Walter A. "Engineering in the Sciences of Life and Man," in *Listen to Leaders in Engineering.* Atlanta: Tupper and Love, 1965.

Rosenblith, Walter A., and Jerome B. Wiesner. "Norbert Wiener, From Philosophy to Mathematics to Biology: The Life Sciences and Cybernetics." *The Journal of Nervous and Mental Disease, 140,* (1), 1965.

Scott, Otto J. *The Creative Ordeal, The Story of Raytheon.* New York: Atheneum, 1974.

Severn, Bill. *The Long and Short of It, Five Thousand Years of Fun and Fury over Hair.* New York: David McKay, 1971.

Shillaber, Caroline. *School of Architecture and Planning, 1861–1961*. Cambridge: M.I.T. Press, 1963.

Shrock, Robert R. *The Geologists Crosby of Boston*. Cambridge: M.I.T. Press, 1972.

Sloan, Alfred P., Jr. *Adventures of a White-Collar Man*. Garden City: Doubleday, Doran, 1941.

———. *My Years With General Motors*. Garden City: Doubleday, 1964.

Smyth, Henry DeWolf. *Atomic Energy for Military Purposes*. Princeton: Princeton University Press, 1948.

Snyder, Benson R. *The Hidden Curriculum*. New York: Knopf, 1971.

Stratton, Julius A. *Science and the Educated Man*. Cambridge: M.I.T. Press, 1966.

Struble, William. "How the Idea of M.I.T. Was Born." *The Boston Sunday Globe,* April 2, 1961.

Sullivan, Louis H. *The Autobiography of an Idea*. New York: Dover Publications, 1956.

Wiener, Norbert. *Ex-Prodigy*. New York: Simon & Schuster, 1953.

———. *I Am a Mathematician*. Garden City: Doubleday, 1956.

———. *The Human Use of Human Beings*. Boston: Houghton Mifflin, 1950.

Wiesner, Jerome B. *Where Science and Politics Meet*. New York: McGraw-Hill Book Company, 1961–1965.

Wildes, Karl L. "Electrical Engineering at M.I.T." Unpublished ms., 1971–1975.

Woodbury, David O. *Elihu Thomson, Beloved Scientist*. Boston: Museum of Science, 1960.

———. *Let Erma Do It, The Full Story of Automation*. New York: Harcourt, Brace, 1956.

Yarmolinsky, Adam. *The Military Establishment*. New York: Harper & Row, 1971.

Zilg, Gerard Colby. *Du Pont, Behind the Nylon Curtain*. Englewood Cliffs, N.J.: Prentice-Hall, 1974.

Picture Credits

Most of the photographs were provided by the M.I.T. Historical Collections or by the M.I.T. News Office and most photographic prints were made by the M.I.T. Graphic Arts Service. Whenever possible, photographers are credited and other sources indicated. Many of the pictures first appeared in *Technology Review*.

Index